A V

The Prisoner of War Diary

of

John Davies Jones

Transcribed by Mair Harris and Robin Davies

Published by Saron Publishing in 2021

ISBN-13: paperback 978-1-913297-18-3
Ebook 978-1-913297-19-0

Cover designed by a friend

Saron Publishers
Pwllmeyrick House
Mamhilad
Mon
NP4 8RG

www.saronpublishers.co.uk
info@saronpublishers.co.uk
Follow us on Facebook and Twitter

Dedication

Remembering Dad
and Those Who Fought in Bomber Command

The bomber war was fought by aircrew of which many were in their late teens or early twenties. One in four was from Canada, Australia or New Zealand. During the whole war, 51% of aircrew were killed on operations. One moment they could be on a bombing raid and a few hours later, could be back enjoying a beer in the pub. Alternatively, they could be shot down and die or, as Dad did, survive and become a POW.

Front Cover: *Back row: F/S Bob Kendall, Sgt Barry Howarth*
Front row: Sgt George Thomson, F/S John Jones, A/F/O Norman Overend
Kneeling: Sgt Spagatner, Sgt Harry Beverton
Back Cover: *F/S John Jones (left) with unknown trainees in Canada*

Preface

In 2010, *The Big Lottery Fund Heroes Return 2* paid for Dad and George to return to Mannheim to visit the graves of the two who didn't make it.[1]

Dad later related in an article:

'Our skipper Norman Overend, a 22-year-old New Zealander, and Harry Beverton, were both killed. The skipper went down with the plane and could have tried flipping her to try and get out himself. The mid-gunner jumped out with us but he was never seen again. I was only 22 but I was one of the oldest crew members on the plane. That's how young some of the crew were.'[2]

Dad and George and the remaining three crew members met often over the years, with their wives.[3] Dad and George always sent each other Christmas cards with a penguin on, which was their mascot. George is 96 and the only one still alive and living in Glasgow. We are in touch.

It has been my privilege to share the Log Book. And with love for my Dad I end,

Mair
September 2021

John, pictured left with George. Their families remained firm friends after the war until John's death in February 2017

John left and George at the memorial graves of Pilot Norman Overend and Air Gunner Harry Beverton

Visit to the Durnbach cemetery paid for Heroes Return 2 in 2011. John pictured left, German hotel manager and fellow crew member George Thomson

Inside cover of the War Time Log

New Owner
F/S JONES, J. D. 573430
6 PENYGRAIG TERRACE,
PONTYPOOL,
MON
WALES

Obtained from previous owner for 40 cigs (American)[1]

John Davies Jones at home in 2010

How to Read the Diary

John made the original Diary very difficult to read, in case the Germans found them. This is Mair's explanation of how she and Robin had to read it. The original end-of-page notes are included in bold italics throughout the transcript itself to give authenticity, though the entries themselves have been transcribed in chronological order:

Commence Page 1 – Read first Paragraph, then turn to thick Grey Pages for the Page Heading 'My Last Trip – FRANKFURT'. This is a double page plus the final page but there are five grey pages in between.

Now return to Page 1 and the Diary continues on odd-numbered pages until Page 53. Then we have to miss the heavy grey pages with special items. The Diary then continues on Page 55, still on odd pages until Page 111. Now go back to Page 2 but turn the book upside down and read back through the even pages up to Page 54. Miss the grey pages and the Diary continues on Page 56. Then there is a missed page 58. Recommence Page 60 until Page 86 – FINIS

Original spelling, capitals and syntax have been retained, although commas have been added for readability. Any inconsistencies reflect the same in the original text. The maps proved difficult to reproduce as many places have changed their names with the changing face of Europe but are recreated to the best of our ability.

Shot Down

Tuesday Sept 12th 1944

England[1] – very nice English summer afternoon – found out early that we're 'on ops'. Briefed at 17:00 hrs. Found out that target was Frankfurt. Details of trip to be entered later.

Turn to centre grey *pages*

The Air crew: Standing: Sgt 1 Spagatner (A/G), A/F/O Norman Overend (Pilot), Sgt Harry Beverton (A/G)
Seated: F/S Johnnie Jones (B/A), F/S Bob Kendall (W/Op), Sgt Barry Howarth (F/E), Sgt George Thompson (Nav)[2]

My Last Trip[3] – FRANKFURT[4]

We had quite a nice trip out and as we flew over France very low, about 50–100 Ft, the people were waving joyously and we waved back. Meanwhile, it was hard for Jock to navigate owing to the varying speed and the winds on deck level so variable. Dusk fell and it was soon dark. Meanwhile we had climbed to height. I saw ahead, right in our path, bays of searchlights and flak and realised that it was Mannheim. I knew that we had to turn before arriving there so asked Jock, 'How long before we turn?' He answered, 'Shortly or very soon' – to that effect. I mentioned to Norman that when we turned, we should have Mannheim on our right. We carried on the same track and the search lights and flak were getting nearer and I realised that if we didn't turn soon, Mannheim would be on our left instead of right and I knew how unhealthy this could be, having flown around the Mannheim searchlights before and then it was one of the best displays I had seen. I reminded Norman once again about which side we should be on. I think George gave him our new course. Then Harry gave us 'Port Go' and we corkscrewed onto the resumed course but only for a short time. Then I heard the beginning of machine gun fire or cannon fire and Spaggy (Rear Gunner) yelled something about 'Corkscrew'.[5]

This was the last thing I heard over the intercom for, as I later discovered, my intercom had been shot away. Meanwhile the kite was full of smoke and my Bomb Aimer's compartment was very bad and one could hardly breathe. There were flames licking out of the Bomb Bay and I yelled over the intercom to tell the skipper and rest of crew. It was then I realised my intercom was dead. I thought maybe my plug had come out but putting my hand down the lead, I found it had been shot away. I opened the small inspection door from my compartment to the Bomb Bay and saw the flames licking around and going like hell. Staggered up the steps to the skipper. This was all one could do as the smoke was so great. Yelled to him to 'Open the Bomb Doors'. He nodded, then I rushed back down to the Bomb Compartment and jettisoned all our bombs, 'cookie' as well.[6]

The smoke died down quite a lot and I grabbed the extinguisher and pushed as much of myself (as possible) through the bomb bay inspection door and tried to put the flames out first in the bomb bay. To my idea, I thought they were dying down a bit, but the next I knew was Barry coming down the steps with his chute fastened on. I yelled for another extinguisher, but he answered back, 'Bail Out'. I started looking for my chute and it was up ahead right in the nose. I went to grab it and meanwhile started opening the escape hatch. Barry gave me a hand with the hatch and it went. I still had to fix my chute on, so told Barry to go, also George who was just behind him. They did and meanwhile I fixed my chute on and jumped. When I left the kite, I had my hand on the carry handle of the chute and it was some seconds when I was in the air before I realised this and then I grabbed the Release handle and yanked. I was prepared for a big tug but altho' there was one, it was not as great as expected. Then instead of the rushing of air, I found myself suspended and swinging gracefully. Then the search lights on me. I forgot to say that they had the kite held in them for quite a while after we were hit and before we bailed out. I felt very alone up there and with the searchlights on me, was expecting flak to come up at me or for a fighter to come and shoot me down. I realised I must be getting near the ground although descending down was not apparent. So I started looking down, saw the deck below but could make out 'nothing'. Then there was a hell of a bump and I hit the deck. It was totally unexpected and I must have let out quite a yell on impact. Released myself from the chute and collapsed same. Looked around for any of the others but saw none. Saw the kite burning and heard the ammunition exploding quite a way away. Buried my chute and Mae West, got rid of my stripes and boot tops and started walking.

John as a new RAF recruit, aged 16, 20th April 1938

John earning wings in Canada

Training in Canada, John seated centre wearing a flying jacket

My Diary Starts

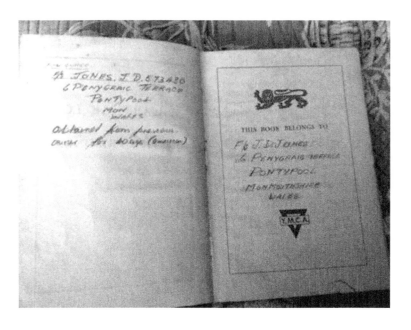

John's POW Log Book inside the first pages. A non-smoker all his life he exchanged 40 American cigarettes for the diary[1]

From here, my diary starts but regarding the episode just described, when I read it over, it seems like a long time but it was actually very short. Also the fact that my intercom was shot off means that I missed everything that the Skipper and the rest of the crew said. Also I could not tell them how everything was going down with me and in the Bomb Bay, as personally I thought the fire was going out but who knows. Anyway, this is all I can remember and I should very much like to have the rest of the crew's versions.

Found and Interrogation

'Bailed out' – Found the experience not so gruelling as expected, although I did hit the deck a bit hard. Did necessary[1] and started walking – walked about 10 mls then tried to sleep in a wood – very cold and damp, but carried on until 11:00 hrs when the wood suddenly seemed to be invaded by people, all who had some kind of uniform with horrible looking German eagles on some part or other. I got more or less surrounded and was left only one opening – to give myself up. Did so and was then asked plenty of questions by one railway man (who, by the way, have the smartest uniform in the country) and by a youth of 17 who was a cadet in the army. I learnt from them that the reason for the sudden invasion of 'my wood' was solely due to the fact that the Yanks were making a daylight raid on Mannheim where they came from and whence I would be taken and as soon as the warning went, the inhabitants (of Mannheim) piled aboard a cattle train and came out of the town into the woods until the all clear went. This is what happened and I found myself in a cattle truck going to Mannheim. Had to change trains and picked up a military guard. I was obliged to carry two white enamel buckets on the next train and through Mannheim and I felt very humiliated.[2]

Taken to R.T.O[3] and had to await a suitable guard. Then I was taken to an aerodrome just on the outskirts of Mannheim, having had to walk or jump on trams to get through the town here. I got slung into a cell and started to find my bearings. Found that there were about 8 or 10 cells and some were occupied. Heard someone pacing up and down in the next cell and could tell that it was 'Spaggy', our A.G's walk. Made myself known to him and he told me Bob was in the next cell up to him. Felt much happier. They gave me a blanket so settled down for the night's sleep – 11:45 awakened and found they had slung a Yank in the cell with me – slept on.

Sept 14th Thursday

My breakfast was the first meal since Tuesday – was two pieces of bread and a small amount of jam. Had a short interrogation in the morning by a woman and found that the number in the cells had increased to about 18. Went back to cell and had two chaps put in, one a Squadron Leader, the other an Australian – rather a lot for one wooden bed and one blanket, but lasted the night OK, even if cold.

Sept 15th Friday

Were woken up early and told we were moving, but not told where.

Given nothing to eat. Walked about a mile to station and finally got on train. Travelled for about three hours and finally got off the train in a suburban station of Frankfurt. Taken off station and told that we had to wait for transport, as owing to the RAF raid on Frankfurt two nights before, the lines were all bombed. Waited 5 hrs, then at about six pm, the guards decided we would have to walk. There were 23 of us and none of us had eaten that day, also two of the Yanks were badly injured so we were not feeling too good, but we had to walk it. Bob and I carried one of the Yanks most of the way, about 10 mls, and it was not too nice walking through the streets as the town was literally to the ground. Finally arrived at the station, we had to catch the next train. It was about 8:30 and found we had to wait until 10pm for the train and had to wait outside the station in the street. Now the trouble started and the angry population started ganging up on us with remarks 'Let's get them now' and 'Schweinhund' and were trying to push past the guards which were only four men – made us feel very much on edge as one of our chaps could speak German and was repeating what they said. Also their action of spitting at us didn't help. Lucky for us, it was dusk and therefore the crowd was not as big as it might have been earlier. Nevertheless, we were ready to make a bit of a fight for it. Anyway, got on the train and arrived at our destination just before mid-night, namely 'Dulag Luft' (Air Interrogation).[4] Put in a cell with five others, 4 Yanks and one RAF who I knew from Canada. Had nothing to eat and had to spend the night on a stool so it was not too comfortable.

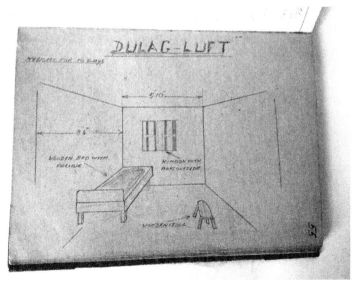

John's drawing of the cell at the interrogation camp

Sept 16th Saturday

I was woken up about 6:30 with two pieces of bread, small amount of jam and water. During the morning, some of the rest of the chaps were taken out and did not return. Finally I was called and I left two behind in the cell. Had a short interrogation whence he tried to get all the 'Gen' out of me but failed. Then I was taken to be photographed, finger prints, all my Gen taken down about myself regarding build etc. Then I was searched and had to strip right off. Took nearly everything I had except Battle Dress, shirt, hanky. I was very annoyed when they took my yellow silk scarf and just said 'Confiscated'. Was taken to a room, perhaps it should be called a 'Cell'. The dimensions of same were 5ft 10 ins. x 8ft 4 ins. with one bed, one stool and a beaker for holding water, also one Blanket. There was a window with plenty of iron bars on the outside. The door was locked and a guard outside and when we wanted to 'Go', you knocked and the Guard accompanied you to same and 'watched and waited'. The wooden blackout shutters were put up at 7:30pm approx. and I settled down to a welcome sleep, even if the wooden bed was rather hard.

Sept 17th Sunday

Had my shoes thrust in about 6:30, having had to put them out the night before. Breakfast 7 am, usual 2 slices of bread and an inkling of jam, also some coffee which I attempted to drink but after one sup reverted to water. Day started passing slowly. Had a bowl of some kind of soup. The most one can say about it, it was hot. This was about 11:30. The day now started passing very slowly and then about 1:30pm, I was handed over for another interrogation. Different int. officer. He started off quite nice trying to pump for all the 'Gen'. He got nowhere. Tried telling me what the Geneva rules said about giving information and that name, No. and rank was not enough – I knew he was Bullshitting me. In the end, he got very annoyed and started yelling and saying I was a spy and he would hand me over to the Gestapo. He said I could not prove my identity – This was partly correct as I did not have my Identity Discs and I had discarded my stripes, Brevet and Epaulets and all I had was my identity card. Told me to think it over and he would see me tomorrow. Returned to my room and another two pieces of bread and a spot of margarine which was not too good and then my shoes were taken away and the shutters down and once more to bed.

Sept 18th Monday

Same routine, had an interrogation by the same officer. Much the same as before, but lost his temper quite early. Went back to cell and had no sooner sat down when I was taken out again to the interrogator. He says he is very dissatisfied with me and was now going to take me to the C.O. Took me in the other office and then this other chap who seemed to have quite a high rank had a 'go' interrogating. Started off by saying I was an agent and not RAF and that he would hand me over to the Gestapo. Also showed me photos of what they did to prisoners – Tried to frighten me into talking but 'he had had it'. Really got wild in the end and started yelling orders at me, and in the end sent for the guard to take me back and just about raised the dead with a yell of 'GET OUT'. Back in my cell and once again the old routine – 'Shoes outside' etc.

Tuesday Sept 19th

This is my fourth day in solitary (*Added later* – little did I realise that I would be in there for another six days without being able to speak to anyone except ask the guard outside the door, what the time was). Time starts passing very slowly and I find that the best way to pass the time is to think back upon various episodes of my life and reminisce on these parts for as long as possible. But in time one's thoughts revert back to thinking on how long you are going to be kept in here and what happened to the rest of the crew. I naturally think a great deal of Pat and Mair and can imagine how much Pat is worrying and I sincerely hope I can get word to her soon.[5]

Wed Sept 20th

Still the same old routine, also same food exactly.
    Breakfast – 2 pieces of bread and jam.
    Dinner – bowl of thin soup.
    Tea (Supper) 2 pieces of bread and marg.
    Doesn't exactly tend to make one fat.

Thursday Sept 21st

Still in solitary and am getting quite a beard on, not having shaved for 12 days.

Friday Sept 22nd

I have now been here a week, and six days of it in solitary and five days since I saw an interrogation officer.

Saturday Sept 23rd

What can one say about these days? They are all the same – empty. I think my morale has dropped at least 50%.

Sunday 24th Sept

This is my ninth day and 7 days since being interrogated and I'm getting rather worried and shall be very glad to see someone and speak to them. Saw George but could not speak.

Monday 25th Sept

Called for Interrogation about 3pm, and he asked me if I would 'come clean'. Said 'No'. He then gave me some 'Gen' about the kite and our crew. Told me there was one dead in the aircraft. Christ knows where he got all the 'Gen' from, but he had. He then told me I would be leaving for a POW camp next day and this did make me feel much better. About six o'clock the guard came in and told me I would be moving over to the other part of the camp for the night. This I did and the first two RAF I ran into were George and Barry and was I glad to see them. Naturally we all started speaking 13 to the dozen. They told me they had been on the loose 8 days before being caught about 20 miles from the border. Found out that we were sleeping about 12 in a billet for the night and were moving to another camp at 6am. Big lot of Para Troopers came in who had been captured in Holland.[6]

Wetzlar

P.O.W. Transit Camp at Wetzlar

Tuesday 26th Sept

Set off under plenty of guards at 7am for the station. About 100 of us, mostly paratroopers and Yanks. About 8 RAF.

Waited at the station until 10am for the train and then when we got in one, was very much crushed, although I was lucky and shared a short seat with 6 other guys. Arrived at a station called WIESBADEN at about 2:30pm and little did we realise that we would wait there on the open platform for five hours until 7:30pm and it was cold. Finally, we got sorted out with Yank aircrew and got on a bus. The para-troops boarded another train. Arrived at a camp called Wetzlar about 8pm.[1] First got searched, photographed, fingerprints etc. and then we got a kitbag with towel, pants, vests, toothbrush, razor etc. which we were very glad to get. Then we got taken to a shower bath and had three minutes under it and was it good. The first time we had washed since shot down which was two weeks ago. Then we got taken into the Mess Hall and had a good meal of mash and corned beef and good coffee. Did we feel good. We had 60 cigs in our kitbag and were the lads who smoked glad to get them. Gave mine to George and Barry. Next, we got taken over to the billets which were very good with 3 tier bunks – about 6 of these in a room. I got put in a room with Bob – he had come there two days before. Got to bed and felt much better.

Wednesday 27th September

Breakfast was at eight o'clock so did not have to get up too early. The meals here are very good due to the fact that we get Red Cross parcels which are all pooled and cooked in the mess and the cooks are British or Yank prisoners.[2] The senior allied officer is a Yank colonel who is a good sort. We find out that this is only a Transit Camp and we should be going on to a permanent camp in a few days. Got a book from the library which is not too bad. Sent home to Pat my first card and I hope that it gets there quickly.

Thursday 28th Sept

I have been eating quite well and we would like to stay here till the end of the war but this is not very likely as it is only a Transit Camp so we will be going soon. In the billet with us are some boys who have been in the hands of the Gestapo and what they have gone through and what they would do to repay the Jerries is not nice to repeat. They really look physical wrecks, white and terribly thin. Some of them have been in the hands of the Gestapo for six or eight months. Also in the billet were some Frenchmen who were captured in Italy. None of them could speak any English but we got on well together.

Friday 29th Sept

Told that we would be moving to a permanent camp that evening and it should take about 5 days' travelling. Had one last meal at Wetzlar about four o'clock and then went and got searched and afterwards marched down to the station. There were about 48 of us, about 50% RAF and 50% Glider Pilots. Boarded the special carriages which were not too bad if we had not had nine in there instead of six which they were built for.

We each got given a Red Cross parcel which by the way are wizard and contain something like this:–

Tin of powdered milk, Tin of corned beef, Spam or Treat,[3] Tin of butter, Tin of orange juice or Jam, 2 bars of chocolate, 100 cigs, Box of cheese, Box of biscuits, Tin of salmon, A pkt of prunes or raisins, Pkt of sugar, Tin of coffee.

Two decided to sleep on Roof Racks

We settled down for the night.

Saturday 30th Sept

Did not sleep very much, also the train did not move very far except being shunted around. Travelling during the day was not too bad. Jock and I decided to share our parcels so as not to waste or have to eat the perishables more quickly as the tins were opened. Decided to sleep on the rack and fixed it up quite nice with cardboard and kitbag.

Sunday 1st Oct

Had a good sleep on the rack, even if cold. The train was making good time. The reason for it being such a long journey is that the transport system in Germany is completely 'Buggered up' with RAF bombing!

Monday 2nd Oct

Slept on rack ok. Told during the day that we would get to the place tonight but would have to stay night on the train. Had a wash today, the first since we left Wetzlar as there is no water on the train and we just managed to get a wash in whilst we were stopped.

Tuesday 3ʳᵈ Oct

Found we had arrived in 'BANKAU' overnight. The camp guards came down for us at 9 o'clock and we started marching to Bankau camp.[4]

Bankau POW Camp (Stalag VII)

Bankau

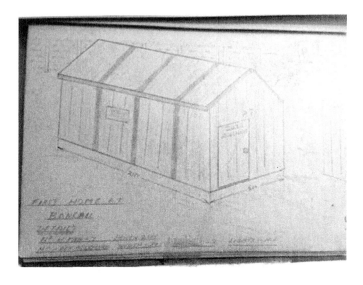

John's pencil sketch of the first hut at Bankau POW camp.

Tuesday Oct 3rd

First day at my new permanent camp was about ¾ hr walk from the rlwy station. Got buggered around for a while. Then once again photographed, fingerprints etc and finally given Hut number to go in. Found that all the huts were like dog kennels about 6ft high. We were given a paper palliasse and had to fill it with straw, and that was our bed. Found the other six chaps in the hut good types and started eating and sharing all the Red Cross parcels. The rest of the chaps were: Jock (from London), Tommy (same), Cliff (Australia), Mo (Weston), George (Lincoln) and Arthur (London copper).

Wed Oct 4th

Started looking around, getting bits of Gen etc, finding out where everything is. Also saw quite a number of chaps I knew before in Canada and back in England.[1] Got a pair of boots and a Great Coat given me.

Thursday Oct 5th

Had a game of football for the Division (There are eight Divisions, about 1000 men all told). Did not play so good owing to unfitness, also new boots. We drew 3-3. Falling in with this prison camp routine quite well. We have two parades a day at 9am and 4:30pm and there's not much 'Bull' attached to them.

Friday Oct 6th

Just the usual day. Did some washing. Found it rather difficult to do same in cold water.

Saturday Oct 7th

Start of third 'Test Match' between Australia and England. England have won two so far.

———

Have now decided to make entries in here once a week and put down all pertaining to that week.

Sunday 8th to 15th Oct

Went to church on Sunday. During the week, everyone is talking about the move down to the new billets which are supposed to be much better. Also the Geneva Delegates who came here said that we should be out of these billets and in Winter ones before Nov 1st.

Australia won the Test Match. Moved down to the new billets on the Friday. There are 14 men in each room but at the moment there are only 4 double decker beds so eight men can sleep there, rest on the deck. We cut the cards for the beds – I won one – consider myself very lucky. Wrote a card and letter to Pat. Find these billets much better and warmer, although there are no stoves or fires. The other seven chaps we have with us seem ok.

Sunday 15th-22nd Oct

Getting more used to new billets and started getting organised on a Rugby Pitch. Got all rugger bods together and representative from each Division who said each Div. could turn out a team which means 8 teams. Also intend to run Internationals Games with England, Wales, Australia and maybe Scotland and Ireland.

Yours Truly was elected chairman of Camp Rugger Committee. Had a concert on the Saturday night in the mess hall and it was quite good. Jerries stopped us singing 'God save the King' so decided to sing 'Land of Hope and Glory' instead.

'Mo', one of the chaps in the room, had about five letters from home. He was shot down in June and this was his first letter. The rest of the chaps were shot down about the same time but none have heard yet, so guess I will have to wait quite a while.

Forgot to mention there is one chap here who was taken prisoner about the same time as me in the room, namely 'George'. He is a glider pilot in the army and was captured in the Arnhem 'Do'.

Sunday 22nd-29th Oct

Went to church and the preacher who, by the way, is a pilot, age about 23, was at Leeds Uni studying for the church, gave a very good sermon. Find it much better to listen to one of your own fellows give a sermon than some of the older ones you get back home.

Football pitch is not progressing too good owing to lack of shovels etc. Not a great deal happened of interest during the week. Some of the chaps who were shot down in July had their first letters from home. Myself and another fellow made a fireplace for the room out of some bricks but Jerries took it 'off of' us two days later. Damn well time we had some stoves in as the weather is getting cold. Wrote a letter to Pat also a card to

Turn to Page 55

dad and mam. Hope by now that they all know I am ok. I am having a bit of trouble with my eyes. We have now formed a Welsh Club here and it's quite good. We meet every Sunday evening at eight o'clock and discuss various things.

Sunday 29th Oct-Nov 5th

At the Welsh Club meeting on Sunday, we decided to form a choir and during the week we had three practices and it should turn out quite good. We are about 50 Welsh boys strong in the club and about 20 in the choir which is not too bad. Had a discussion on 'Home Rule' for Wales but at the end the majority voted against. It's decided to have speakers next week for

(1) Welsh Industries (2) Education (3) Agriculture. I was elected to speak on Industry so shall have to prepare something.

Go to Page 55

Page 55
John's note in Header: Cont. from Page 53

Wrote to Pat on the Sunday but found it rather difficult to fathom out what one can put down with both English and German censoring. We had a dance on the Wed, no girls of course but some of the chaps dressed up and some really put it over, even if they did accentuate 'Piccadilly' resemblances but I think most enjoyed it.[2]

We got the Stove put in the billet which, believe me, was not too soon, also the rest of the beds which were really necessary. Two of the chaps from our room have gone into hospital with chills of some sort.

Sunday Nov 5th-12th

Had the usual Welsh Club meeting on Sunday and I spoke on 'Industry', think my speech was rather rough but the others seemed to think it ok. Have decided to start the meeting with Cwm Rhondda and close with the Welsh National Anthem 'in

Welsh'.[3] Had quite a few choir practices and it's coming along quite well. I have been having a bad attack of diarrhoea and have seen the medical staff but the treatment given me has not done me a lot of good as I've had it for seven days, also my eyes are not too good but I had the same trouble back home last Winter. Had our first fall of snow but it was not a great deal and cleared soon. Saw a German Chimney Sweep and it was really funny as they still wear a top hat, tails and white Dicky etc. and he came into the camp as the morning parade was on and everyone was in an uproar.

On the Saturday, it was 'Remembrance Day' and we had a parade and short prayer. A trumpeter played the 'Last Post' and we observed the 2 mins silence. Afraid all one's thoughts went back as far as the last war but thinking of the people back home, also of chaps we knew and were with us this war but unfortunately have been killed. Was wondering what had happened to Norman and Harry and hope to hell they are ok, but as one looks at facts, it doesn't seem too hopeful. Feel very sorry for Harry's wife and child, nevertheless we shall not give up hope.

Sunday 12th-19th

In the Welsh Club, we had a Gramophone Recital which was quite good. As a visitor, we had the new Padre who is an Army Captain and is about 6ft 6in tall, in fact a Rowing Blue.

He is the only British Officer here and seems a very good type.

On the Sunday afternoon, we had choir practice, also practice for solos and duets. The conductor wants me to sing a solo but I'm not too keen. So far, we have been practising with a piano-accordion but now we have the piano room and we have found a very good pianist who is L.R.A.M. and has had quite an amount of experience with choirs so we are very lucky.[4]

On Monday, we had our first real snow on the camp and we now have a very good stage, bit small but with footlights, scenery, curtains etc. Only thing wrong, the seating capacity is not too great – about 200 men so it means each show has to run for 6 evenings for the whole camp to see it. Anyway, the show was a great success and comprised mainly of seven turns; the Band, small amusing sketches and ended up with the play 'Rookery Nook' by Ben Travers.[5] This was done very well and the chaps taking female parts were really good and the costumes were very good. Everyone really enjoyed it.

Started Welsh classes on Tuesday and we have two periods a week allotted to it. Should like to learn to speak it fluently, but I doubt this very much.

Had a big fall of snow and had a bit of sport with snow fights.

Sunday 19th-26th

Had a two-hour choir practice on Tuesday and it went over very well. Also, this new pianist is very good, also helps a lot with the conducting.

Started practising 'Sweet and Low', think Tennyson wrote the words and it's a very good number.[6] Our weekly club meeting went off well with a chap Lloyd giving us the 'Gen' on the Police Force. Spoke very well and interestingly but still don't think I would like to join the PF, too much like the 'Services'. Also, there was a chap from Newport who gave three monologues of Stanley Holloway and he is very good.[7] At last I've managed to get the rugby cracking. I think I have put it down before that I am chairman of the Camp Rugger so have to arrange most of the necessaries. One very good thing is that we now have jerseys and shorts but the great shortage is boots of which we haven't any. Nevertheless, I got all the practice games off on Saturday and it went down very well with bags of spectators even when it was raining and after the day's play, bags of chaps said they were glad to see rugger going and I think we shall have better support than soccer. We both use the same pitch but we have it all day Wednesday and Sat. morning. The soccer have it the rest of the time. There are eight divisions here and from these we can get six teams for Inter-Div competition which is quite good considering there are only about 150 in each Div. I'm in hut No.8 and captain of the Div Rugger. We won our trial game 6-3 pts, quite a good game and think I played fairly good. Have the makings of a good team in our Div.

Saturday night, I went to the newly formed 'Dickens Fellowship' and really enjoyed it. The present reading is 'Pickwick Papers' and is very amusing. Quite homely in there, sitting around the stove with one of the fellows reading. During the week went to the Welsh Classes and did quite an amount but it's not so easy and needs quite a lot of 'Homework'.

According to the news, the big advance has started and we are all keeping our fingers crossed for it. This week the B——— Germans cut our coal ration by half. Also, when we get Red Cross Parcels, they open the top of the tin so that it has to be eaten straight away.

Sunday 26th-Dec 3rd

In the Club Meeting, we had our new padre give us a talk on 'Holidaying in Scotland'. He is a very good speaker and it was very interesting. Still keeping the Welsh Class up and progressing slowly. During the beginning of the week, I had the Division Rugby team out practising and on the Wednesday, we played a League Game with 8 Div. We have a very good team but were very lucky to win by 3pts-0. Think I played a good enough game. We have decided to have a game Gt Britain v Dominions so we have to get the selectors together to pick the team.[8]

I went to a concert on Thurs night and it was very good. The main feature was the accordion Band which is really good. Also there was one chap dressed up as a girl calling himself Georgina and did he look good. Best impersonation I've seen and the rest of the chaps thought the same.

Had Red Cross Parcels in the week which was very lucky as we were on the last issue. So now we have enough to last us over to the week after Christmas at ½ a parcel per man per week. This means 50 cigs a fortnight, also one bar of chocolate for the same length of time.

Played the Dominions on Sat and were very unlucky to lose by 3pts-0. It was a very hard game and the Brit Team played well. I think I played alright and was actually over the line once for a try but the Ref thought different. I was Capt. of Brit Team.

Our potato ration is to be cut down by 25% which is not too good.[9] As it is, we only get about 4 spuds a day. So we have to hope for the best. – B – these Germans. Had a British Medical Officer come to the camp, he is an Army type but seems ok.

Dec 3rd-10th

In the Welsh Club meeting on Sunday, we had a chap give a talk on CHINA up until 1938. He had been a reporter there and was not too bad but was not what one would term a 'Good Speaker'. On Tuesday, went to see or perhaps one should say 'Hear' 'Journeys End' by R C Sherriff.[10] It was acted behind closed curtains so was just like a radio broadcast. It was Very good and extremely well-acted, especially the chap who took on Stanhope. His name is Terry Cooke and I shall have to keep his name in mind for when I get home as he is excellent. Also this week on Thursday, we had our first cinema show namely 'Corsican Brothers' was quite good but no sound at all as the sound track on the film is ——— Worn out.[11]

Played rugger on Wed. and were unfortunate to lose 7pts-6pts.

Dec 10th-17th

Had an inspection by our MO, ok. Our coal ration is very small and we can't have the fire on all day.

Jesus, is it cold. We have really had a bad bout of coldness this week and quite a big fall of snow which is still on the ground, about 9in. deep. According to all reports, it should stay like this until about March, so we can expect to be COLD. We have only two blankets which are not too warm, in fact rather thin. Two nights before the snow, it was absolutely freezing and we were all awake for most of the night. Another bad point is the fact that to keep as warm as possible, we have to keep the window closed and you can imagine what the taste in one's mouth is like with 16 men sleeping in our room which is not too big.

Enough Grumbling – We have had a picture show called 'Life Begins for Andy Hardy' which was very good and the sound this time was quite good.[12] We also had a Band Show but this was not so hot, in fact pretty deadly. There was only one good turn and that was a Maori singing native songs. In the Welsh Club meeting, we had a quiz and a Housey-Housey game and the prizes were 5 cigs per time.

During the last week, I have made friends with a Welsh lad from Merthyr. His name is Emrys Harris and he's quite a good type and very amusing. Hope to see something of him when we get home. The snow seems to have finished the rugby, which is rather a bind.

Most of the chaps got mail from home but they were shot down in June.

I expect I'll have to wait a while. I feel sorry for Arthur as he is the only one of chaps who have been here a while and has not heard. He is 38 and married with two children and he feels it keenly – but nothing can be done as it's a matter of luck how many letters or how quick they get through.

Dec 17th-24th

In the Welsh Club on Sunday, we had Emrys Harris speak on Coal Mining. I was surprised at the number of Welsh chaps who were slightly ignorant of mining. He spoke really well and he enlightened me in places. Our parcel stock is getting rather low and we've just enough to last us until Wednesday the 27th. We saw a flick 'Dixie Dugan' which was very amusing.[13] This is the last flick we have, goodness knows when we shall get another.

The weather is still very cold and there's plenty of ice around. We had another two chaps come into the room – one

Canadian and one Yorkshireman. This makes our room total up to 18 which is very crowded. The Jerries this week have been boasting of an advance they are supposed to be making on the front but we naturally don't believe it as they publish such a lot of propaganda. On Wednesday, most of the lads received mail and were really in good spirits. Personally felt rather 'cheesed' and according to the length of time for the mail to get here, I don't expect any before about March. We had a new 'Man of Confidence' this week, the old one being voted out.[14] The new one Ron Meads is a damn good type and I hope he makes a good job of it

Well, Christmas is drawing very near and we are not feeling too downhearted but I would not say that this is the best place to spend it. We baked two cakes for Xmas day and they seem to have turned out alright.

Dec 24th-31st Dec

CHRISTMAS EVE

On Thursday I played soccer for the Welsh Team against a combined team of S. Africa, Rhodesia & France. We lost 3-2 but think we were unlucky we did not play so good – had some more snow on Thursday night but not a great deal. During the week, we have had quite a number of choir practices for New Year's Eve when we are singing at a Camp Concert so I hope we are good for that night. Buried the Canadian on Saturday and twelve men from the camp went to the funeral.

CHRISTMAS DAY

We had to get up quite early as parade was at 8a.m. This was the only parade of the day, so we were quite lucky. Breakfast went down quite well and for a change, we felt a bit full. After parade, we went back to bed as there was nothing really organised on for the morning. In the afternoon, we watched a football match between the two best teams on the camp and it was very good and the weather was wizard and not too cold but had that Christmassy feel in it and a drop of scotch or some such thing would have made it even better. I went to the church service but found it cold in there. There was nothing fixed up for the evening but in the corridor of one of the Divisions was an impromptu concert which we went along to, and at least it passed the evening away before lights out, which was the normal time 10p.m. I wrote a card to Pat. Afraid I did a lot of reminiscing during the day and naturally was imagining what they were doing at home and what I would be doing with them. One thing the menu was very good and well cooked and very enjoyable and for once I was 'full'. At the conclusion of the day, decided that, for a P.O.W. Christmas, we did quite well.

Dec 31st–6th Jan

We had the Welsh Club meeting at eight but it consisted only of a brief resume of what the club had done since its forming and how well we had progressed.

After the meeting, we went to the Camp Concert in the theatre which was organised by the Scots, and we, the Welsh Choir, were singing on the stage for 20 mins. The show didn't start until 10.15p.m. as the idea was to see the New Year in. Our help to the programme went on at 11p.m. and we sang four songs namely, Men of Harlech,[15] Cwm Rhondda, All through the Night[16], Ton y Botel.[17] We had a WIZARD RECEPTION and had to give an encore which was the first mentioned. The rest of the programme was very good and there was a short service from about ten to twelve until the hour, then we had a minute's silence and then Auld Lang Syne. It was a very good evening's enjoyment. One can imagine how much reminiscing and hoping we are doing.

The Man of Confidence received a note to say that there were 4,000 Red Cross Parcels on the way from Geneva so I hope they get here quickly. These Argentine parcels we had were quite good and made some good meals out of it.[18]

The best being the oatmeal biscuits which, after being soaked in water for an hour, swell to about twice their size and then fry them as pancakes and are they good.

Jan 7th-14th 1945

Sunday night, instead of our usual meeting, we had a 'Quiz' with another club, namely 'Midlands Club'. It was good fun but we lost 39pts-35 but I think everyone enjoyed it. Have an ulcer in my mouth and is rather sore. Only hope it clears up soon. We (the Choir) are going in a show with Leo Maki and his Accordion Band in about a month so we have to get 'crackin'! [19] There was a Panto on this week and it was very good and a big laugh. I am still taking Welsh and progressing slowly. Everyone seems happy this week as the reports sound good. We had some very cold nights this week with a dry wind blowing from the East. During the week, I went to a talk by the Medical Officer on 'Sexology' and he was very good and very enlightening [20]. I think most of the fellows learnt something. This week I started going down to the forest and collecting wood which the Russian Prisoners have cut down. It's not far but there are ten of us on the party and three armed German guards take us down. It feels good to be the other side of the wire, if only for a brief spell as this is the first time I have been outside since I came here. With some of the new BODS who came in this week was a chap from Cwmbran and he knows Pontypool well, so I expect I have to see more of him when we get home. On Wednesday night about midnight, the Jerries had a big search in 8 Division hut and unluckily found 'The Tunnel' which had been going in there. It shook everyone as quite an amount had been done to it and was very ingeniously carried out. Spaggy was in on it but we don't know yet what is going to happen to the chaps concerned.[21]

I have not made an entry for quite a while, the reason being that we have been on 'The March'.[22] When I describe the March, I shall do so day by day, but at the moment shall attempt to describe the panic back at BANKAU before we actually started. By the way, at the moment, I am writing this on top of a hay stack in a rather draughty barn at a place called Plauswitz.

To resume, the 'Big Panic' started on Wed 17th Jan and we were told that we were moving, evacuating to SAGAN (Officers camp).[23]

The reason is that 'Joe' was getting near and there were bags of rumours.[24] We wanted to stay and hope that the Russians would get here quickly and release us. No such luck. But we were told that we were marching which did not sound too good. We were also told that if anyone tried to escape on the march, FIVE other men would be shot. We were paraded numerous times and once we were off then with our kit on, lined up ready to move off but we were told to go back to the billets. Meanwhile, there were bags of rumours on how far the Russians are away but we can only rely on the 'Cocoa' which is bound to be a couple of days old.[25] Anyway, we can hear bags of gunfire, also see flashes at night. As it is intended for us to march, bags of kit to dispense with, but we are still pretty heavily loaded. Thursday night about 8pm, there was an Air Raid and the camp lights were on till the last minute, then we heard the aircraft - after a short time, there was a big explosion followed by 4 or 5 more and we who were looking out of the window (silly people) saw that it was a string of bombs which overshot the camp and landed a short distance from the wire. We were soon on the deck but there was no more near activity but we heard plenty in the distance. We were told that we were moving off at 3:30am but as this was about the dozenth time we had been told, we did not know what to think but went and laid down with our clothes on and a couple of blankets over us. This was the third night we had done this, so we were getting rather cheesed.

The Long March

A drawing of Australian POWs being marched through Germany during the winter of 1944-45

The March FINALE (We hope)[1]

Friday Jan 19th 3:30am

What a morning, it will remain in my memory for ages. We were called on parade at four and there was a cold wind blowing, it was absolutely bitter. We were buggered around, standing and waiting, and did not move off until after six. We could see bags of gun flashes in the distance, not near enough to stop us moving. We passed through Kreutzberg and it was getting light. The roads were full of evacuees, also troops. Everything was being pulled by horses and during the day, the number of dead horses we saw on the side of the road was enormous. Was the going hard or not? The roads were covered with snow and ice and the lads were feeling done in. Bags of cases and kitbags were being thrown away and I felt like doing the same but kept on to it. We finally knocked off marching at 5:00pm and were slung in a small barn for the night – about 200 of us. Forgot to say there were about 1400 of us who started off – wonder how many will finish.[2] The place we stayed the night was Wintawelde. We were so tired that we just slung a blanket over us and went to sleep. The Padre was in the same barn as us and said a prayer. Do we need it.

John's note in Header: Distance marched first day 25-28 km

Saturday 20th Jan

We were roused at 4am and were on the march about 5:30. The feet and body were really sore and stiff after a rest and I had a couple of blisters on my feet. We marched until about 11am and then we were all put in a brick factory. Meanwhile, I had dispensed with some of my kit including my flying shoes – I was sorry to part with them but they were much too heavy. We were told that we more than likely be moving in the evening and marching all night. This really shook us as we were all in but had a rest, also lit a fire and had a hot drink of cocoa. This was the first hot drink since we left. My feet were soaking wet as it's impossible to keep the snow out.[3] The rumours flashing around were tremendous, some being that JOE had taken Bankau and was very near, also that the guards were all out for deserting – Don't know how true they were but we started off at 8pm. The idea, we were told, was to cross the river ODER which the Jerries would make a defence line. The distance we had to go they would not tell us. It was expected to be quite a long one. Our spirits were not too high at the start but by the end – well!

Distance travelled 2nd day 12 kilos, Total 40 kilos

Cold was dreadful and the breath on our collars was well frozen, also our hair.[4] We were tired but when we rested, we froze up. Men were falling out right and left. I felt like doing the same but saw how useless it was as one would only be left behind as the cart carrying the sick was well overfull. It was ages before we got to the Oder and it was HELL. We crossed the river at about 4:30am and were very tired and just managed to drag one leg in front of the other. We came to a village the other side about 6 kilos and we expected to stay there, but we were told that there was no room for us there and had to march another 7 kilos. This nearly knocked us out but nothing could be done about it and we had to make ourselves march the rest. It was deadly, and when we finally got there, we just about collapsed in the barn. Accommodation was bad, also it was cold but we were too tired to worry about it. We had a cup of coffee and then went under. It was estimated the night march was 41 kilo and with the 12 earlier on made it 53 in a day - night. 44 miles, the place we stayed at was Rosenwald.

John's note in Header: Distance at night 41 kilos. Total 81 approx.

Monday Jan 22nd

1:30am, as one can see, we were called very early – found that my boots were frozen. Forgot to say that the M.O. gave a lecture or a bit of a talk on morale etc, ended up by saying 'Remember

44

you are British' ———B———. Before we moved off, there were bags of chaps who were heading to stay and it ended up in quite a 'do'. The Camp Leader got up and said he thought it best for everyone to move and stick together. Then someone jumped up and said it was madness to march along roads with the possibility of bombing and strafing by Russian aircraft. Anyway, we got out but some stayed in the barn, but not for long as the Jerries came in and fired their revolvers and threatened to shoot if they did not get out instantly. They did but there were quite a number jumped the party there. Arrived at Schonweld about 1 or 2pm.[5] The places we passed through were : Alsemar, Keradswalau, Zindel, Bankau la, Kachendorf. We had to wait outside the barn while they turned out the cows. Then we went in and put some fresh straw down and slept where they had been. We made some hot tea and cocoa, also we were lucky enough to find some carrots. We were now beginning to get a bit hungry and the Jerries had not given us any bread ration since we left Bankau when they gave us two days' rations. Regarding the marching, we still felt tired but were getting used to it but one can't do it on an empty stomach. Got a small packet of biscuits.

John's note in Header: Distance travelled 25 kilos, Total 106 kilos.

Tuesday 23rd Jan

(I am now in a railway truck.)

Had a good night sleep but were up quite early about 5am and were on the march. We first walked about 3 K the way we came and were in the area of Breig but did not pass through it. Arrived at Wansen Heideisdorf about 4 or 5 in the afternoon and first of all, we had a very cold barn, but later crammed ourselves in with 4 other lads in a beast house with some cattle still in but had pens around them. Myself, I slept in a feed trough at the side of the stall. During the night, a cow managed to get over the bales and amongst the chaps sleeping – caused a bit of a panic, but they managed to get it back into the stall after a time.

Wednesday 24th Jan

Stayed the night at Wasfen, also next day and night. We had our first bread issue and it didn't come too soon either. We were lucky enough to find or perhaps one should say stole some flour out of one of the farm wagons. At things like this, one becomes rather adept at getting wood for fire. We got some tea on, also we had some potatoes which we roasted and also we made little balls of the flour after wetting it first and put them on the embers of the fire, they roasted quite nice with some butter on. Had my first wash and cleaned my teeth the first since starting. I felt much better.

Thursday 25th Jan

Had to get up at 3am and were on the road about five. From the time one gets up to the actual time of really starting marching, we take between an hour and a half and two hours as it's quite a big job to get about 1600 men on the march and also for them to be checked off. My feet, by the way, have not been really dry since leaving Bankau and to get the socks anywhere near dry, one had to go to bed in them. This is not too bad but should imagine that some time in the future, it will lead to some kind of rheumatism or some such thing.[6] Told that we had to walk 30k so imagine that we are in for a hell of time. It was a hell of a long walk, especially the last 10k. But we arrived all ok. The place we came to was Heidersdorf.

Because the diary is now upside down, the Header has become the 'Footer': Distance 4th day 22 K, Total 128 K.
This is now Page 4

Friday 26th Jan

We rested here the day but it was not too good as we were billeted in a big barn but our bed place was in the alleyway and one got trodden on all the time. We now have to make a double bed with another chap to keep warm. I made mine with Arthur and find it a bit warmer. Jock was feeling really sick and had a bad night and had to be taken to the other barn which was the hospital and was kept there.

Sat 27th Jan

We left Heidersdorf at 11am and in a way were glad to get on the march as it was not too good where we were. We had to go 21 kilos and then we came to a place Paffendorf and this time, we had a bit better barn but it was nothing exceptional.

Note in 'Footer': 5th Day – 30 K, Total 155 K

Page 6

Sunday 28th Jan

Left Paffendorf at 4am and were told we only had to walk 18 kilos which shouldn't be too bad. It was fairly cold but we soon got warm by setting off early. The place was Standorf. We went on the scrounge straight away and I climbed on to a cart on the farm and found about a 14 lb bag of flour of some sort.

Managed to smuggle it back to the loft we were sleeping in. Did not have chance to cook any of it but had a hot brew of tea that evening. The billet was rather cold and there was a big hole in the wall which did not help.

Monday 29th Jan

Did not move in the morning – had an issue of hard rations, biscuits and corned dog which I must admit was not too bad. Found that we had a night march to do, everyone said No. The M.O and Camp Leader said it was impossible to the German Commandant, but it was no use.

Note in 'Footer': Distance travelled 6th day – 21km, Total 179 km

We were on parade about 4pm and moved off about 5:30. There was a bit of a wind blowing and it started to snow, then woof – a blizzard started and it was deadly. The blizzard was nearly dead against and there were drifts 3 or 4ft. deep which had to be gone through. It was hellish and nearly everyone was exhausted but had to keep going for if you fell out, you had had it. Saw one dead German guard lying dead on the side but no one took any notice. This was definitely the worst march and when we arrived at our destination, Petrowitch, which was about 5:30am, we were nearly dead. The billeting was bad and it was nearly 8am before we had a place to lie down. We simply collapsed for about 6 hrs.

30th-31st Jan

We rested here and during the day, made Welsh Cakes out of the flour and they were quite good. Were told that we had another march to do before we got transport. Forgot to say before that they promised us the same before we got here.

1st Feb

Left Petruwitch for Prauswitz, a distance of 14km. Stayed here till the 5th but were very badly off for food although we were in a warm barn. Roasted spuds, also cooked some barley which they issued to us. We were really getting stale here and starving. They gave 2 days' rations for train journey.

Note in 'Footer': Distance travelled 8th day 29 km, Total 208 km

Train Journey

Feb 5ᵗʰ Monday

We had reveille at Petrowitch at 4:30am but it was well after that before we actually got started – about 6:30. We had had quite a lay off from marching and this told on us and we were soon tired. We only had to walk about 10km to the railway siding and it really told on us and by the time we got there, it was 9:40. We got slung into the trucks, ordinary railway trucks, and there were 55 of us in each truck, so one can imagine what it was like. There was hardly standing room and as one tried to sit down, it was deadly. We left Goldberg about 1pm but did not travel very far in the afternoon. In the evening, we had quite a good run and got into Sagan railway station about 9:30pm. We were expecting to keep travelling all the time but here we were disappointed for we stayed the night in the siding there and it was terrible. One had to spend the night sitting on a blanket with your head on your knees and it's surprising how quickly one gets stiff, also with someone else's head on your knees does not help. There was no light in the truck so we were in pretty well darkness from 4:30 in the afternoon till 6:30 next morning. Another bad point was that a couple of chaps had the diarrhoea and after a few times of having to unlock then lock the door, the Poston (guards) were not keen to open it when we shouted for him, it meant that they just had to do same in their trousers. Apparently, every truck was in the same condition so I considered myself lucky not to be suffering from same.

Tuesday 6ᵗʰ Feb

Found that a couple of chaps had dropped off at Sagan. The time we had actually set off in the train was about 7am but we did not move very far or very fast. Our food now is pretty low and most of the chaps have run out – We only had food enough for yesterday. Myself, I'm feeling rather weakish. When I stand up, my head starts to swim around. Our food is really low and our ration will only hold out for today. So we are hoping the journey is not too long. During our overnight stay at Sagan, two of the fellows in the truck 'jumped off' – one was Spaggy, our rear gunner.

They have left it a bit late for jumping off, but I hope they are ok. We did not travel very far or very fast and stopped at a place called ————. The time being about 4pm. Everyone is feeling really cheesed off, in fact, morale is pretty low.

Wednesday 7ᵗʰ Feb

My Birthday, what a place to spend it. All I have to eat is a small crust and this has to last until we get there. We started off about 10am but did not travel very far and had many long stops. These days, one reminisces more than ever, especially on home and wonder what Pat and Mair are doing. Also, everyone talks of food and what they are going to eat when they get home. Another thing, the way the Bloody Jerries have treated us on the move has been dreadful and I'm afraid the lads will have no sympathy for any German after these sorts of things, like the guards changing one or two loaves of bread for gold watches or rings don't help. Also, the way the guards are provided for and the Commandant says he can't get food for the P.O.Ws. Lots of other things also, too numerous to put down which will take a long time to be forgotten. Today, everyone is out of food, even the fellows who had the odd crust and everyone is edgy. Tempers are very frayed and blokes go up in the air over nothing – of course, this can only be expected. During the day, we do not travel very far but about mid-night we arrived at our destination, at least the railway station place is Luckenwald and we have to go to a camp somewhere outside it. They will not unload us at night but have to wait until the morning. I can't see us walking very far in the condition we are as everyone is getting so weak. Only hope they give us something to eat before we set out but this is very doubtful. – So ends my 23rd birthday and I only hope I never have to spend another one like it.

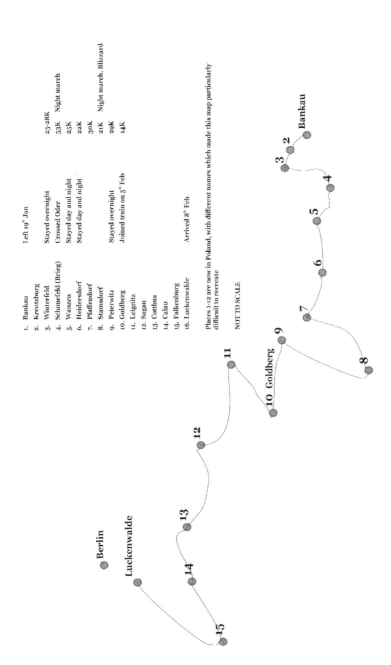

1. Bankau — Left 19ᵗʰ Jan
2. Kreutzburg
3. Winterfeld — Stayed overnight — 25-28K
4. Schonefeld (Brieg) — Crossed Oder — 53K — Night march
5. Wanzen — Stayed day and night — 25K
6. Heidersdorf — Stayed day and night — 22K
7. Pfaffendorf — 30K
8. Stamsdorf
9. Peterwitz — Stayed overnight — 21K — Night march. Blizzard
10. Goldberg — Joined train on 5ᵗʰ Feb — 29K
11. Leignitz — 14K
12. Sagan
13. Cottbus
14. Calau
15. Falkenburg
16. Luckenwalde — Arrived 8ᵗʰ Feb

Places 1-12 are now in Poland, with different names which made this map particularly difficult to recreate

NOT TO SCALE

Bankau

Goldberg

Berlin

Luckenwalde

53

Luckenwalde

Thursday 8th Feb

We are kept hanging on in the trucks until 11am and then they unload us and not many can hardly walk. They bugger us around the station for a while, then start walking for the camp – still with nothing to eat. Lucky we did not have to walk long – about 2 or 3 km. We finally arrive and find we have to have a shower before we eat. I know we badly need a bath but wish they would let everyone eat first. Takes ages for us to get one but manage to make a fairly hot drink of tea whilst in the shower. Next we are taken to a billet which is a big hall which has some bales of straw in it. There were about 850 of us put into it and it seemed like heaven to sit down and rest on the straw. Of course, it was a bit of a crush to find a spot but one managed to get a fairly decent one. Pretty soon afterwards, there was a cupful of barley soup with about 4 spuds. It was the army boys here who issued it to us, it was simply wizard. Afterwards we had another cup of soup with a wee bit of meat in and we really began to feel a bit stronger. They still didn't give us any bread but we had more now than we had eaten all the trip – we bedded down quite early and were soon asleep.

Friday 9th Feb

Got up about 9 o-clock but there was nothing doing regarding food just then. Had a shave –the first for 3 weeks so one can imagine what I looked like. We were still very weak and as one stood up, you just about keeled over and it took up too much energy to even put one's coat on. Looked around outside a bit and found 1500 officers from Sagan in the other compound and there was plenty of yelling over from the boys who saw chaps of their crew, also ones they knew. I didn't see anyone I knew and was a bit disappointed. They seemed to have bags of cigarettes and were throwing them over to the boys. This went well for a while but then the guards came and moved everyone away and one couldn't even speak to them. We had a parade about 10.30a.m to check on our Ration and strength and about eleven or twelve, we had our bread ration plus some dripping, we had two days issue of bread but the B_____ still owe us plenty but we never had it. Bread ration per day 1/5 loaf.

We had a cup and half of barley soup about 3p.m. plus 5 or 6 spuds. Also some coffee about 7p.m. this was the lot for the day. I ate most of my bread and felt a bit fuller, but far from strong. It's surprising how thin I have got and when I was bathing the other day, my ribs stuck out miles, also my cheeks are sunk in. Everyone is more or less the same, also there are a hell of a lot down sick. Went to sleep about 8p.m. and slept OK until about 5a.m.

Sat Feb 10th

We found out in the morning that the end of the billet where we were sleeping was wanted for sick patients of whom there are plenty since coming here and the results of starvation is beginning to tell. We packed up our stuff early in the morning to Move but it was six in the evening before we actually did. The place we moved to is not too bad but just as crowded but we have some straw to lie on so one can't grumble too much. The 'Cocoa' is plentiful here, also good and we get it twice a day. Rumours going around that we are moving on Monday or Tuesday but nothing is definite. Had the usual day's ration of 1/5th of loaf, 5 or 6 spuds, cup full of soup and cup of Jerry tea which is pretty deadly. Some of the chaps saw Jock who is in hospital and left us on the March at Schweinite and travelled on by train to Sagan and then by train to here. He did OK as they had Red Cross parcels. As many as they wanted as they were evacuating, also plenty of cigs.

Sunday Feb 11th

Forgot to say before that the title to this camp is Stammlager 111A and is actually an Army camp.[1]

The main people on here are FRENCH and they are really running the rackets and as usual are a lot of bloody rogues. They run the cookhouse, parcel and clothing store, boots etc. In fact, everything. They are even still getting Red Cross Parcels and we are damn well starving. They are full out for trading bread for rings and watches, also cigs. We hope to do a bit of trading ourselves with them. The rest of the Bods here are Americans, Serbs and Russians. Besides us and the R.A.F officers are about 300 Irish soldiers. They have been here about a year and were sorted out from different camps because they were Irish but they don't know why. They are damned good types and do their best for us but they have not a lot to give. Went down to the Hosp. to see Jock in the evening and he does look ill but seems cheery enough. Cocoa was good.

Monday Feb 12th

Today, Robert collapsed and is in very bad shape, don't know what is wrong yet but hope he is OK. Went down to see Jock and also Darky who is sleeping besides him. The lights were off for about 2 hours but don't know why. Felt pretty rough today, going dizzy when I stand up. Bags of chaps going down sick, some with dysentery and quite a lot have diarrhoea and stomach trouble but are too weak to combat same. Laid in bed most of the day so as to conserve some energy as impossible to do much on these rations.

Tuesday Feb 13th

Found out that Robert is very ill and has pneumonia, only hope he pulls through. In the hospital, everyone has been walking on their toes because of his condition. Myself, I feel a bit better. We got an issue of 12 cigs today which had been taken from unclaimed parcel, changed 10 of mine for a ration of bread so consider myself lucky. During the night there were air raids all the time on Berlin, forgot to say before that we are only 30 miles south of Berlin so have to put up with all the air raid warnings etc. Started reading the New Testament, which I have carried with me since leaving Bankau. Arthur is trying to change his watch for bread and wants one whole loaf for himself and wants to share the rest, two between we other five, only hope it comes off.

Wednesday Feb 14th

Today is when they expect the Red Cross parcels but none arrived and myself, I doubt very much we have much chance of them. The funny part, if one can call it funny, is that the British or Americans who provide the Red X parcels have none whatsoever, whilst the French (the b___) Serbs, Poles etc. here have them – makes one think. Robert is much better, at least has passed the crisis but is very weak.

The chances of changing Arty's watch are not too bad but can only get 2½ loaves, in fact they gave us ½ a loaf towards it which really helped.

Thursday Feb 15th

Today has been a big exchange day and myself, I have got rid of my watch. Sounds bad but conditions are bad and we are very hungry. One of the Irish boys did the exchanging for me with the French or Serbs. Whoever it was does not interest me very much but what I got for it did. The exchange was for 5 civilian loaves which is equal to 6 military loaves. I naturally had regrets parting with the watch but what can one do – I can buy a watch when I get home but I'm damned sure I can't buy my health. Of the five, I have about 1½ for myself, giving the chap who put over the exchange a piece and keeping one whole for myself, and then dividing the other three loaves left between the rest of the six of us. It was the only thing to do as we are all hungry and we six have shared pretty well all so far. Norman earlier traded his gold signet ring which his family gave to him for his 21st and was a very good one for 2¼ loaves and he kept one and shared the rest among us so what can one do. Forgot to say I gave George, my navigator, a piece as I realise how hungry he is and I'm sure he'd do the same for me if he had a chance. We had good news that our day's ration of bread was going to be cut and instead of us being five to a loaf, there was to be 7½ men's rations in each loaf. Supposed to compensate for this was an issue of flour which is about ¼ or ¹/₃ of a cup. What a life. Cocoa was good.

Friday Feb 16th

The main matter of interest today was that the 'Protecting Power' was here. He was Swiss and looked over the quarters and the M.O. and Camp Leader gave him all our 'Gen'. He asked a couple of chaps in our billet to strip, they did so and did they look wrecks of men and we must all be more or less in the same condition. One can't imagine the state and condition of all the men here, at least who were in Bankau with us. The sick parades are enormous and this morning lasted 5½ hours so one can imagine how many men a service M.O. can get through in that time. Dysentery is bad, stomach trouble etc. great, all due to mainly lack of food. No one has an ounce of colour and find difficulty in walking even back and for to the latrine and lie down most of the time to save their energy, then, when they stand up, their head just whirls around and one has to grab something to hold oneself up. Men collapse in the billet, on parade, latrine etc. and have to be carried to the M.O. Morale is very low but one of the worst things happened yesterday, two men were caught stealing another man's ration of bread. This is very bad and I would not like to be in their shoes as every detail on it has been handed over to the Protecting Power and will be forwarded on home. Think that the maximum sentence is 14 years' PENAL SERVITUDE. In the afternoon after the visit, there was a conference with the M.O., Camp Leader and the Swiss official, then about 4 p.m. the M.O. and C.L. came around the billets and gave us what Gen they had. It was not good as the P. Power told us to expect worse yet and that the chances of the Red Cross parcels were not good. He admitted that conditions were appalling and that the rations were bad. He would do his best to improve same and was seeing the Commandant that evening but he could not promise anything good but as said before, he would do his best. The M.O. also shot a line about self-discipline, morale etc. and that it was getting worse due to the men alone and that the dysentery was caused more through the men's own fault when on the March, eating sugar beet and other things. Why the hell didn't he tell us at the time about what effects might be expected from beet instead of putting the fault on the men afterwards? Also he hasn't had cause himself to eat it on the march because he himself and the rest of the hospital staff, Camp Leader and his gang of officials, also the cookhouse staff have not yet starved as much as us and also, if he and the Camp Leader showed more ESPRIT DE CORPS and exerted more discipline on the march, he might be allowed to speak the way he did, that also goes for the Camp Leader, both whom to my idea have neither the authoritative force necessary or can command respect enough to be in charge of 1,500 men.

Physically myself, I am feeling much better but nowhere near being fit. Everyone seems to think the war to be over in a month or so, two months at the outside. I only hope they are right. The Cocoa these days is good. Naturally lying in bed most of the day, I think of home most of the time, of Pat and Mair and what they are doing and longing to see them. Also of food and I'm sure when I do get home, I shall be eating all the time, meanwhile one can just visualise different dishes, mainly steak, eggs, chips, porridge, bacon, different types of cakes, in fact, everything, but one thing that seems to stick out is the steak and kidney pudding Gran & Aunty May used to make, followed by steamed spotted dick pudding & jam with white sauce. I intend having all of these things I visualise when I finally do get home and think I will be eating all the time and drinking tea, coffee and cocoa with bags of milk and sugar. Drink has taken a back place at the moment but imagine I shall have some good celebrations but don't think I shall drink as much as before I was shot down. These last few days I have spent an appreciable amount of time with my Navigator, George and we talk of old times, also of the crew etc.

Saturday 18th February

I forgot to mention the other day that the Frenchmen in charge of the cookhouse had been slung in the 'Cooler' as it had been discovered that they were working a racket and keeping some of our rations for themselves. There were a truckload and a trailer full of Red Cross parcels came in today but as one might guess, they were for the Poles here. Once again, they were British & American parcels, in fact, that's the only kind there are. Broke into my 10mark bill today which I changed for a bar of soap. Back home at the moment, there are 15 marks to £1 so that's worth about 15 shillings. Bought myself some toothpaste – 2 marks and these pencils 30 pfennigs each so I am left with about 7 marks. Went down to the hospital and Jock is getting better, so is Darky but there is another chap in there I know, namely Jimmy Davies, who was chairman of the Welsh Club who is there with a bad attack of rheumatism and is really ill.

Sunday 19th Feb

Life is beginning to get very monotonous here with more or less lying down on the straw with no books to read or anything to do. Here, we have to get up quite early as the morning parade is at 7.15a.m. This makes the day rather long – the other parade is at 4.30p.m. Today we are rather lucky as we got issued a ¼ of loaf per man instead of a 1/5th. I actually meant to go to the church service today but at the time, I was attempting to make a cake or something out of a cup of flour and a bit of my sugar and marg. issue. It didn't turn out too bad but there was not much of it.

Monday 20th Feb

Today I decided to have my second shave since being here – it was 10 days since I had my last one. There has been talk about our RAF Officers being given 354 Red Cross parcels by the Norwegian officers. It will be a damn bad show if they keep them as they are in much fitter condition than us and did not have to march here, also when they left Sagan, they had more parcels given them, also as many cigs. as they wanted, in fact, when we got here, they still had bags left, in fact they still have. The Group Capt. in charge complained the other day that the discipline and morale of the NCOs in this compound was low. I'm sure that if him and his b———— officers had been through what we have, their morale or flag-waving would not be high. Anyway, we have nothing definitive as yet as to what they are going to do with them. Myself, I am feeling much better than when I came here but I am damn sure I haven't put on any of the weight I lost on the march and I am not likely to until I get home.

Tuesday 21st Feb

Today, it will be our turn to fetch the rations and the general fatigues around the billet. We had to carry the soup and spuds for 350 men from the cookhouse to the billet, a distance about 300 yds but in the condition we are in, it seemed like 10 miles. One thing, it was something to do and occupy the time. Gave myself a cold bath, (that's all one can have), under the tap and then put on some clean underclothes I had washed here – felt much better. Norman is not feeling too good today, also myself, my stomach is a bit deadly. Once again in the evening, the M.O. came and gave a 'Pep talk'. Rather fed up with hearing him on about morale and I'm sure everyone else is. The parcel climax came today with regard to the officers – they sent over 35 parcels for our sick boys of whom there are quite an amount. Also an explanatory letter which dealt to the effect that actually they had been given 500 parcels by the Norwegians but were all for Allied Officers, and as there were Polish, Americans etc. amongst them, also as there were 5,000 American NCOs here, it wouldn't be correct to give them to us – sounds alright on paper but I 'have my doubts'. The Cocoa was not as good as usual.

Wednesday 22nd Feb

Robert has been moved down to the main camp hospital which is a good sign as he will get better treatment there, also the M.O. said he would not move him there until he was stronger so therefore he must be stronger. I managed to borrow a book off Paddy Heron – it's short amusing stories. Spent the evening talking to Walter & Jonny (who by the way comes from Varteg[2]), mainly as usual about food.

Thursday 23rd Feb

I had a tinge of a sore throat when I woke up this morning and hope it does not persist. We got a small bit of German sausage meat instead of margarine today so I saved my potatoes and made a bit of a stew out of it in the evening, not much but helped. I think I shall keep this daily entry up as expect something big to happen to us soon. Today, there are plenty of rumours that we are going to move again but we have heard nothing authentic. Sent letter to Pat but doubt she will get it.

Friday 24th Feb

Today is Red Letter Day, we had the Red Cross parcels given to us by the officers divided amongst us. What a game, it worked out that, after the Hosp had taken some of the parcels, there were about 20 left and then worked out about 30 or 40 men to a parcel – one can imagine how much that meant. I got 1/10 of a block of butter (1lb block) this was the lot. Another good point was that each man got 22 cigs, these came from unclaimed personal parcels, shall keep mine for changing sometime. Also, about 2 oz. of tobacco, gave mine to George. Today the Cocoa was very good. Today is my mother's birthday – many happy returns.

Saturday 25th February

We were told today that 2,000 R. Cross parcels had been dispatched from Lubeck for this camp, also that a further consignment were being dispatched immediately just for Stalag Luft 7 which should be a good thing if they ever get here. In the evening, we had a game of Solo. The Cocoa was exceedingly good.

Sunday 26th Feb

Had a bit of gen off a chap who has not been shot down long that all P.O.W. of Bomber Command were to be flown home and guaranteed that they were to be in England 2 weeks after Peace is declared and that we have 5 days getting kitted up etc. and sent on indefinite leave with £10 and when recalled, to have medicals, convalescence, and later for them to decide on discharging you or training for a ground trade. Today, we saved all our soup and spuds and made a bigger 'dixie' full of soup at tea time. Was much better and hotter. The Cocoa is still good. Did not go to church. Had an air raid – we have been having these every night and sometimes in the day for quite a while, the reason being that we are so close to Berlin.

Monday 26th Feb

During the night, there was an air raid on Berlin and we could see the Red and Green flares going down and hear the aircraft and bombs – hope it was a good prang. All day, we seem to be talking of food all the day and what we are going to have back home. Think I shall have to collect recipes as I intend trying my hand at a few different dishes. Today, the Cocoa was quite good. My physical condition is not too bad but is definitely not improving and won't do so on these rations. One still gets periods of blacking out when you stand up. I spend a lot of time during the day wondering and thinking about what will happen to us when we get home. Hope we get a good leave as I intend having a good rest, also to give Pat a good holiday, also I shall go to Slough to my mother's and with a spot of luck to Coventry. Should like to spend a week or so at the coast, Torquay or N. Wales somewhere, providing we have good weather.

Tuesday 27th Feb

We had a couple of Air Raids during the day but we never saw any actual thing. The weather is not too good – drizzly rain and low clouds but hope it clears up soon and gives 'Joe' and our boys a good chance. I managed to borrow a book today but it's not too good. Saw some of the Welsh chaps today and they are thinking of having a meeting for St. David's Day on March 1st. The Cocoa was quite good and hope it keeps so. One of the Jerry 'ferrets' had just come back from Dresden, the place which has been getting bombed a lot lately, and he said it's pretty deadly.[3] It's only 70 kms from here and it took him a day and a half to get here so the transport system can't be so good.

Wednesday 28th Feb

Last night, we had three air raid warnings so I expect Berlin had a bad night. Also, we had a notable happening in the camp. During the air raid, a couple of our RAF chaps, well, one Aussie and one Canadian, made a raid on the store at the end of our barracks which contained the Frenchies' R. Cross parcels. This was not the first time and unfortunately for them, there was a Jerry waiting for them. One got shot through the side and back, the other got a flesh wound. They are both in hospital – Christ knows what will be the end of it – Court Martialled at home, I would not like to be in their shoes. Never the less, feel sorry for them as the way the FRENCH are treated here and how well they live compared to us is disgusting and most of the boys have more against them than the Jerries here.

Thursday 1st March St. David's Day

Today the Army took over running us instead of the Luftwaffe – don't know whether it's a turn for the better or worse. Once again, there are Red X parcels in the station for the French, quite an amount, about 9 truck loads, approx. 23,000 parcels. The German Commandant has said we can have ¼ parcel per man but don't know when. But I think there is a bit of a stink being kicked up about the French having them again, especially by the Yanks as there never was too much love between the Yanks & French and there is something to the effect that the French are only supposed to have one American parcel per month, as before France was invaded by us, they also used to get parcels there, the fact and the way they corroborate[4] with the Hun does not help. The weather is getting worse and March has certainly come in with a big wind. Air raids again last night and today Cocoa was not so good as usual. Did some clothes washing, the second time since coming here but it's very hard to get a white towel white with only cold water and only Jerry soap to use on clothes.

Friday 2nd March

This morning, I managed to get some German coffee for 3 cigs. Some had a couple of brews during the day. The Cocoa was WIZARD and hope it keeps so. The majority of chaps seem to think the war will be over in a couple of months still, but that was what we thought when we came here and that's three weeks yesterday. Pity Joe couldn't get cracking again as he is not far away. We were promised a ¼ parcel tomorrow and ¼ on Wednesday, only hope it materialises. Today, we were duty group and had to do all the local fatigues. What a day, a hell of a lot of wind blowing.

Max Schmeling was here yesterday in civvies and quite a number of the boys got his autograph – what the hell for, I don't know.[5]

Saturday 3rd March

RED LETTER DAY or RED X DAY, in other words we got issued a ¼ parcel per man and has the morale gone up. It is not much but it does make a difference. Took a bit of doing to split up but as Norman and I are sharing, it only meant dividing into half. We did not get the issue until late, but we managed to have a cheese and jam sandwich – must get this when I get home. Cocoa was quite good.

Sunday 4th March

Spent most of the day making a 'Smoky Joe' burner which comprises of a couple of big tins with holes and cutaways and is very good for boiling small amounts of water or cooking on with very small pieces of wood. Also made a frying pan out of a couple of tins – surprising what one can make with little tools when one has to. The Cocoa was simply WIZARD. For tea, we made some toast, then had some meat and beans which we cooked on the burner.

Monday 5th March

Had some more snow today, only hope it does not last too long. The boys here seem much happier, now we had a bit of decent food out of the Red X parcels. In the evening, we had a 'Prune Scilly' which comprised of mixing some prunes, sugar, marg, bread and water and boiling up for a while, then put some KLIM milk with it – Tasted WIZARD. [6] The Cocoa was very good.

Tuesday 6th March[7]

Bags of rumours going about parcels being in but nothing definite. The Cocoa is still good. We have a spot of difficulty getting wood but it's surprising where it all comes from.

Wednesday 7th March

What news – there are definitely parcels in the Railway Stn and tomorrow we get a full parcel. The Cocoa is still right on top.

Thursday 'D' Day (Red X Parcels)

Our much mentioned and much looked forward to parcels were given out today and did we feel good – Morale jumped up 100% and although we did not get them until about 4:30, there was bags of it. Cooking going on between then and lights out which these days is about 8p.m. when the Mossies do their usual milk run on Berlin and then during an air raid, all lights are switched off.[8]

Myself, I soon devoured a bar of chocolate, also had coffee with bags of milk & sugar – Went to bed happy.

Friday 9th March

This morning, I went down to the Rugger pitch and had a 'run around', the reason being that the Irish boys were playing the French on Sunday and they had asked me to play for them – felt a bit short of wind but should be O.K. Today the Cocoa was made with 'water crossing' and all feel very good.[9] We ate very well during the day and had a hot cup of chocolate just before settling down for the night. The 'Milk Run' was on as usual last night about the 18th night running.

Saturday 10th March

Felt a wee bit stiff, also had the 'olde trouble'.

Page 56 Upside Down
FROM Page 54

The reason I think is the sudden amount of good food, only hope it does not last too long. The Cocoa still very good and all going well. Norman and I getting along very well sharing the parcels and it's just the right number to have for full parcels. Today we were told we have enough parcels to last another 5 weeks so we have no worries for a while.

Sunday 11th March-18th March

Decided to make entries once a week again. Getting on well with the parcels, also moved into new barrack and now we have beds and there are just 24 of us in a room. Played quite a bit of rugger and organised a RAF team to play the FRENCH. We were very unfit and lost 7-3 pts but we did well. I just missed a drop goal from half way – hit the bar and bounced back. Surprising where one gets the energy from after what we've gone through.

Sunday 19th-26th March

The news is WIZARD and now the water has been crossed everyone is cheerful.[10]

GO TO PAGE 60
Page 60
FROM PAGE 56
CONTINUE THROUGH TO Page 86

April 21st

It's ages since I made a last entry but shall try to catch up – Are we excited and what news. The RUSSIANS are very near here and all our guards and officers in charge have gone and left us. Immediately they had gone, the Senior British officer and some more Officers took charge and started to organise the camp. The Irish Guards are guarding every place of importance as the Russian prisoners have run amok and stealing everything, spuds and food – don't blame them but if they don't look after them, we may be starving before we are liberated. We had a KLIM bash to celebrate. One can't keep still and there's bags of activity with artillery, machine guns and aircraft. Some of the boys swiped some wirelesses and I actually heard the 9 o'clock pips from London. It's hard to describe how one feels and how much we are awaiting the Russians and Yanks, finding it hard to realise that we are so near to going home.

Liberation Day and beyond

From John's Log Book entry

April 22nd - 'Liberation Day'

About 8 am, a Russian armoured car came into the camp and was he cheered – drove down the compound with the chaps hanging all over it. The town at Luckenwalde is supposed to have been taken by the Russians and they are expecting the Yanks anytime. Last night, an aircraft came over and machine gunned us and it was pretty close. About eleven, the Russian Armoured Division entered the camp including bags of big tanks, ARMODILLAS'S, troops who looked quite young, not very smart but bloody fit. What a sight, what cheering, cigarettes being thrown at the left and right.

This is surely the greatest day in the period of the time as a 'GEFANGER', the day which one has looked forward to for so long has arrived.[1] The feeling one gets is hard to describe, also it's difficult to realise that one is now free and no longer are we under the hard rule and 'guardianship' of the German authorities. The exit 'Finale Grande' was very similar to a dog with its tail between its legs, except the speed they left was much faster than the four legged friend could possibly hope to make. The Deutsch left the camp yesterday, Saturday, and immediately the Senior British Officer (s.b.o.) assumed command at the lager camp.

This morning, I was lying dreaming of various things when I heard bags of shouting and cheering, I dived out of bed, through the window and up to the wire, clothed in my underclothes only – there, careering down the road, was a Russian Armoured Car. What a sight to witness, the blood inside you warms up and you give vent to much shouting and cheering. The car was swarmed with Russian Soldiers who were smiling and waving back to us. It carried on down the lager to the Russian Compound and there, it received a tremendous welcome. In a short while, it returned and went out of the camp and back to Luckenwalde to the main force. Everyone was chattering and laughing but never the less we went back to bed for a while but I doubt if anyone slept. Suddenly about 10.30a.m. there was a huge cheer and bags of noise of armoured vehicles and down through the main Camp road came Russian Armoured Column containing huge tanks and large armoured cars bearing massive guns and all were smothered with troops who maybe did not look smart but were young, fit and well-armed.

One of the tanks just put its nose on one of the compound wires and just tore the lot down. A short while after, they all drove back with all the ex-Russian prisoners streaming behind them and they were soon on their way from camp whilst we were told by the Senior British Officer to stay put and wait until the Yanks come. This will be damned good when, if and when they do come, meanwhile everyone is scared that the Jerries will make another push and we are recaptured. This would break most of the fellows' hearts especially the 'Old Kreigies' who have waited so long for this.[2]

May 17th

'T'is month Sunday since we were liberated and yet we are still here. During this month, lots of things have happened and we have had lots of disappointments. Firstly, we were told to stay where we are and not to move as the 'link up' with the Yanks was expected any time and then we should be home right away. This took over a week to occur and then it was quite a way south of here at Torgun, meanwhile, there were numerous rumours, also the Officers were trying to 'Bull'.

Saturday nearly two weeks after Liberation

An American jeep and armoured car came here and said they would have us all out in 48 hours. This sounded good and altered our plans as Norman and I intended buggering off the next day and try and make our way to the Yank lines as the Russians seemed to be doing nothing about us. The next day, about 30 American ambulances came and took away the sick people. Then Monday, the trucks came. The first 25 were for the Yank prisoners and then we were to go every other with the Yanks. But sad to say, something went wrong and although 50-60 trucks came, only about 5 or 6 went back full, the reason being that the Russians objected to our going and they did not have permission – just Red tape. Meanwhile, we were told that everything would be in a couple of days and we would be going home and that permission was got from the Russian H.Q. So we were strung along but during this, chaps were still going on their own and making their way to the Yanks who were up to the ELBE. Then the following Monday, another Convoy of trucks came to take us back, about 70 trucks in all but enough to take all British and Yanks back. They arrived in the evening but we were told it was no good going down as they would not be leaving till the following morning and that they would not go till everyone was aboard. This we nearly all believed and the next morning we went down to the wagons and pitched aboard, but some of the chaps had slept down there overnight and a couple of wagons had gone away early with them. Anyway, we stayed on the trucks about an hour and then the trucks drove from outside the camp into the camp with us on board and we were told to jump off and they would be loaded properly –what a line of bull. They hung around a couple of hours and then drove back out onto the road and stopped – meanwhile, it had flashed around the compound that once again the Russian b———— would not let us go and there was a huge rush across the compound to the road where the trucks were but there were Russians there who would not let you on and brandishing their rifles and guns. Some of us started walking, hoping the lorries would pick us up on the way but a Russian came down the road on his motor bike and firing his revolver – what a scene, meanwhile, as we were walking back, the wagons were going away passing us. I made a rush and leap and got on one and lay on my guts, hoping not to be seen, but farther down the road Russian Officers were searching the trucks and once again, I got slung off and finally returned to camp disgusted and once again the wagons returned empty – what was said and what everyone thinks of the Russians could not be written but I have never seen such an ignorant, dim, scruffy mad lot as these b———. Meanwhile the British Senior Officer, whom nearly everyone is fed up with, tries to introduce more bull – and seems to be able to make a hell of a mess with anything concerning repatriation. The strength of the N.C.O.s here is 650 and before, there were 1,500 so a hell of a lot have gone on their own accord as I said before, I was on my way but when the trucks came, decided to wait for them and unfortunately missed the boat.

May 19th

Today, we were told the good news that we would be moving to HALLE – the other side of the ELBE with the Yanks. We were told that we were going tomorrow and going as far as the Elbe with the Russian trucks and then with American. Everyone cheered up and to top it all, the fact that a dance had been arranged in our Compound and the civilian women, internees, Dutch, Belgian, Czechs, Poles etc. were invited. I went and had a fairly good time but one had to 'Sprechen ze Deutsch' which is the only language one can get along with as they could not speak English and I am damned sure we couldn't speak theirs.

May 20th

At last, we have left the Camp. The trucks came for us about 12 noon and we were soon loaded up and on our way. We travelled most of the way as far as the Elbe on the main auto-bahn, which was rather a silly thing to do as all the bridges along there were blown up, also plenty of large holes in the road and one had to detour through the wood and this took a hell of a time and it would have been much better to have gone on a secondary road but naturally the Russians couldn't see this. It was a lovely day for travelling and my face caught the sun quite an amount. The accommodation in the lorry was good as there were only 25 to a lorry. We arrived at the ELBE about 7p.m. and the main bridge had been blown up and we had to go down the bank some way and then cross over a pontoon bridge constructed by the Yanks. We got out of the Russky trucks, walked over the bridge and climbed into the Yanks' ones and did it feel good to be out of the Russian hands and with the Yanks. We were away very shortly and on our way to Halle airfield. One thing I noticed was that the civilian population on the Yank side of the ELBE seemed happier than with the Russians and were not afraid to be out in the streets and were waving to us. We arrived at HALLE airport about 10.30p.m. and were soon in good billets and asleep and it seemed pretty well organised, we were divided up into groups of 25 as this is the no. of persons for each aircraft.

21ˢᵗ May

Today we had white bread for the first time since leaving ENGLAND and was it good and it tasted like cake.

Friday 23ʳᵈ May

Stayed at Halle longer than expected but it was pretty well organised with pictures and shows. Left there Friday just after lunch and flew in a DAKOTA to BRUSSELS. Took us about

Page 84

3 hrs and it was not a bad trip. We actually landed about 20 mls out of BRUSSELS and lorries took us into the town where we will stay for the night. We were now in R.A.F. and Army hands and they gave us a good welcome. In the town we were taken to a civilian hostel which was very well run and were cleaned up and given RED CROSS issues and cigs. Everyone trying to do something for you. Norman and I went out for the night boozing – had a good time.

Saturday

Had breakfast and then we were taken to another airport and once again, climbed into a Dakota, took off about 12 o'clock and then – BLIGHTY – did it look good, even though there was bags of cloud and rain around – landed at Horsham, nr. Guildford and there they had quite a welcome for us and a big tea arranged and they simply could not do enough for us. From here, we journeyed to Wolverhampton but now having been delivered back to England safely, I considered my P.O.W. days over so

Finis

24th May/45

Pat, Mair and John in Maplethorpe,
near where John was stationed after the war

OPEN LIST OF FOOD AND MEALS I INTEND TO HAVE WHEN HOME

Grape fruit with bags of Sugar

Porridge, bags of milk (Nestles) or syrup

Ham and eggs, sausages and fried tomatoes

Kidneys on toast

Steak, burnt onions, chips, chops, pies–steak and kidney, pork

Roast pork, plenty of soups, peas & broad and kidney beans

Jam pudding, spotted dick with white sauce, Christmas pudding & cake, toast cheese also fresh bread and cheese, poached eggs, coffee and cocoa made with plenty of milk or cream, tin fruit with cream, custard, blancmange, plenty of cold ham with pickles, sauce HP

Stuffed chine (George), apple pie and cream.

Fish & chips, attempt to have a bottle of port or sherry in the house as much as possible to finish the meal off. Plenty of good, assorted pastries also chocolate biscuits, all kinds of biscuits, chocolate log, iced cakes, mince pies and jam tarts, custard tarts, bags of big tarts, Welsh cakes, rice pudding, sago pudding, currant bread, Dundee cake, pancakes with syrup, lemon curd and marmalade. Liver and bacon, apple fritters, waffles and maple syrup, creamed rice with raisins and jam.

Grey: Page 59

TON Y BOTEL

Dyma gariad fel y moroedd
Tosturiaethau fel y lli
Tywysog bywyd pur yn mawr
Marw i brynun bywyd ni
Pwy all beidio â cofio amdano?
Pwy all beidio â thraethu glod?
Dyma gariad nad ân angof
Tra fo nefoedd wen yn bod

OES GAFR ETO?

Oes gafr eto?
Oes heb ei godro?
Ar y creigiau geirwon
Mae'r hen afr yn crwydro
Gafr goch, goch, goch
Ie fingoch, fingoch, fingoch
Foel gynffon goch, foel gynffon goch
Ystlys goch a chynffon
Goch, goch, goch.

Grey: Page 61

Grey: Page 58

Recipes

BANANA TART

Pastry in tin. Layer of crushed banana. Layer of custard. Bake
it. Serve with whipped cream and shredded coconut.

CHOCOLATE BISCUIT CAKE

Plain sweet biscuits and moistened with milk. Layer of thick
chocolate and mixed fruit. Repeat layering until about 2
inches thick. Bake in oven.

HAMBURGERS

Toast bread rolls cut in half. Mince steak and mix with onions
and fried. Place meat on roll with fried tomato, Lettuce, and
beetroot. Replace other halfs of roll thickly butter, warm in
oven serve with chips.

YORKSHIRE PUD

Flour, eggs, milk and salt. Mix up egg & milk into flour. Beat
to even batter. Melt fat (suet fat) in baking dish. Pour in batter
when fat is smoking.

Grey: Page 60

CHOCOLATE SPREAD

¼ lb cocoa, 2 spoons of sugar, 2 of butter. Dry or liquid milk.
Mix thickly stirring to remove lumps. Allow to settle. Pour on.

HAWAIAN WHISK

Mix 2 lemon jellies with 2½ pt size Ideal (evaporated) milk and white of 6 eggs. Add juice of lemon and whisk. Mix in slices of pineapple mix altogether, allow to set. Serve with cream.

DEVILLED EGG SANDWICH

Toast buttered and covered with layers of celery, hard-boiled egg (chopped well), mayonnaise, another layer of celery with buttered toast on top.

BAKED TOMATO

Take a large tomato. Cut off top, remove inside. Break an egg into tomato, put sage, onions, salt and pepper. Replace top and seal well with salt. Bake well until done.

BULLY BEEF or SPAM FRITTERS

Cut slices of bully or Spam and dip into batter of egg and flour. Fry quickly and serve.

TOASTED CHEESE and TOMATO SANDWICH

Toast slice of bread on both sides. Butter well. Lay on strips of cheese (cream) ¼ inch thick, put under grill. Take away and add fresh slices of tomato and on each side dap some sour cream salad dressing. Grill again. Take from under and lay thin strips of side bacon over tomato. Grill again. Serve on crisp lettuce.

BAKED APPLES

Core and fill with raisins and brown sugar–cook. Serve with cream sprinkled with cinnamon.

BOILED ORANGE

Take an orange. Cut off top. Take out inside and juice. Mix up well with raisins and sugar. Put mixture back in orange and add two teaspoons of syrup. Put on top. Steam for 10 mins or more. Eat cold.

BANANA FOAM

Beat up two eggs, vanilla and cream. Mix over crushed bananas. Serve with ice-cream.

BANANA FRITTERS

Split banana. Dip in batter. Roll in biscuit crumbs and fry.

Page 62 grey

APPLED EGG

Fry egg. Fry ¼ slices apple in some fat and place between toast.

BACON + SPUD PUDDING

Make suet dough. Roll flat. Chip up bacon and spud and seasoning. Roll mixture in dough balls & boil.

APPLE CHARLOTTES

Grease dish, put layer of thin bread and butter. Layer of sliced apples & layer of brown sugar. Repeat same. Finish with bread crumbs & brown sugar. Serve with custard or cream.

MEAT LOAF

Take any odd pieces of meat. Mince with onion, parsley & bread crumbs. Add raw beaten egg. Shape like loaf cover with brown sugar & bake. Serve with peas & spuds.

SAVOURY FRITTERS

Fingers of fresh bread with themselves of cheese. Dip in egg batter and fry.

ANGELS on HORSEBACK

Take some sardines, roll in rasher of bacon, pin it with skewer and fry. Serve on toast.

BACON & POTATO OMELETTE

Commence frying chips. Dice up bacon. Beat up eggs into and pour over chips when nearly brown.

APPLE RAISIN BERRY

3 cups of breadcrumbs. 1 cup of seeded raisins, 3 T.S. butter, 3 T.B.S. sugar, ½ cup water, 1 or 2 apples, Cinnamon. Slice apples in greased dish add breadcrumbs. Dot with butter. Cover 1/3 of apple & raisins with sugar. Repeat. Bake in oven.

Distance travelled on The March recorded top and bottom of pages

Page 105	Distance travelled first day	25-28 kilo
Page 107	Distance travelled 2nd day	12 kilo
		Total 40 kilo
Page 109	Distance at night	41 K
		Kilo to date 81 approx
Page 111	Distance travelled	25 K
		Total 106 K
Page 2	4th Day	22 K
		Total 128 K
Page 4	5th Day	30 K
		Total 158 K
Page 6	6th Day	21 K
		Total 179 K

They gave 2 days' ration for train journey

Page 8	Distance travelled 8th Day	29 K
		Total 208 K
Page 9	Distance travelled 9th Day	14 k
		Total 222
Page 10	Total DISTANCE MARCHED 230 K	

Name in WW2	Current Name
Bankau	Bąlków
Winterfeld	Zawiść
Schonfeld	Obórki
Breig	Brzeg
Wansen	Wiązów
Heidersdorf	Lagiewniki
Pfaffendorf	Ksiąnica
Standorf	Stanowice
Petrowitch	Piotrowice
Goldberg	Zlotoryja
Leignitz	Legnica
Sagan	Żagań

Other places remain in Germany with the same names

About John Davies Jones

1922-2017

John aged six, 7th February 1928

John was born on February 7th in Canton, Cardiff. He grew up in Trinant in a family of coal miners, his father and uncles were all rugby and cricket players for Crumlin.

He won a place at Newbridge Grammar School, where he was educated until aged sixteen and in 1938 he joined the RAF as an apprentice. In 1942, he signed on to become aircrew and joined 15 Squadron of the Lancaster bombers. His role on the crew of seven was Bomb Aimer, he directed the pilot until all the bombs were released. It was on their 19th mission that they were shot down.

He met Pat through his cousin, Noreen, who knew Pat's sister Joan. They married in 1943 in Newport, then caught the train and honeymooned for one night in Monmouth and he returned to the RAF station. Mair was born the following year.

After the war ended in 1945, he remained to serve out the time he had signed on for, becoming an Instructor. His aptitude for training served him well as he then went onto Llandrindod Wells Teacher Training College, training in PE, History and Woodwork. All remained loves through his life.

Living with Pat's family in Pontypool, John secured a post at Usk Secondary Modern School, remaining there until it closed and children were sent to Comprehensive schools.

During these years, John and Pat were active in local politics and John played rugby and cricket for Usk teams. They also moved to Mill Street, Usk and near to the cricket field. He became passionately involved in the Roger Edwards Educational Trust, became Secretary of the Rugby club, (eventually became President), served on the WRU for many years, started and ran the Educational Centre evening classes (formerly the school he had taught at), became Mayor and was appointed Education Officer at Usk Prison where he remained until retirement.

He was passionate about rugby, loved cricket, politics, France (he organised rugby trips to France from the 60s until the 90s), enjoyed Bermuda and his grandchildren, as well as other children and young people. He was an interesting raconteur and could converse on many subjects with interest and insight. Though reticent to talk about his POW time, his Log Book gives us an insight into the man and the time.

About Mair Lynn Davies Harris

Having been born in Crickhowell, I was brought up in Pontypool for my primary school years and then Usk for my secondary school years. I trained as a teacher like Dad. I went to Bath College of Education and trained as a Home Economics teacher. I completed one year of teaching in England and then at 22 years of age and with itchy feet, procured a teaching post in Bermuda.

I met my London-born husband in Bermuda and we have been here ever since, except for seven years in the Turks and Caicos islands. Mum and Dad visited us once or twice a year for long periods and Usk became second home for our two children growing up. Every summer holiday was spent with them in Usk and enjoying the close proximity to the cricket field and delicious cricket teas.

We continue to live in Bermuda and now have four grandchildren, three here and one in Scotland. Since Dad's passing, in 2017, we have spent long periods of time at the house in Mill Street and it's been lovely being able to continue my relationship with my home town.

Although I had mentioned the Logbook to Dad a few times, after Robin told me about it, he never gave it to me to read and I didn't push it. After Dad died and I was sorting through things, I found it in a brown envelope. I started it and then couldn't put it down. Thankfully Robin and Dad had marked the pages where to turn to, often back to front or upside down! His 'voice' comes through to me and now to many others.

In October 2020, during a 'lockdown', I decided to post some excerpts from the Wartime Log to FB friends and then, after people were so interested, also to email other friends. The interest generated has culminated in the printing of its entirety. I think Dad would be totally surprised but it is part of history, which he so loved.

About Robin Davies

I am John's youngest cousin. His father was the third oldest of sixteen children and my mum was the youngest. Hence, I was much nearer in age to Mair, than I was to John.

You could say that John and I are of different generations. We are definitely of a different calibre. There is no way that I could have dealt with being a POW in the manner that John did.

Although I was aware of my cousins John, Pat and Mair at a very early age, I'm not sure that I realised John was my cousin. I have fond memories of the occasional picnic at Symonds Yat with my parents, along with John, Pat and Mair. This usually involved a chaotic game of French Cricket.

It wasn't until much later in life that I reconnected with John and Pat. My parents had died and I had become interested in tracing my family history. John was to prove an invaluable source of information and we spent many hours discussing our family tree.

Despite John's father and two of our uncles having been in the army during The Great War, the Second World War was never a topic of discussion, until one day he produced his Diary for me to read. He allowed me to take it home to read, but not before laying down the law to me, as only John could, that I must be extremely careful with it.

John did not wish to talk about his life as a POW but he did trust me to help with setting out and checking the directions which would make the Diary easier for people to follow.

I was extremely honoured when Mair asked me to help her transcribe her father's logbook. Every time I read it, I am in awe of what John and his fellow prisoners had to endure.

About the Publishers

Saron Publishers has been in existence since 2000, producing niche magazines. Our first venture into books took place in 2016 when we published *The Meanderings of Bing* by Tim Harnden-Taylor. Further publications include *Minstrel Magic*, by Eleanor Pritchard, George Mitchell's biography, *Penthusiasm*, a collection of short stories and poems from Penthusiasts, a writing group based in the beautiful town of Usk, and *Frank*, a gentle novel about loss, by Julie Hamill, followed in 2019 by its sequel *Jackie*.

2019 also saw the publication, among others, of Kevin Moore's second book, *Real Murder Investigations – An Insider's View*, which delves in more detail into some cases mentioned in his previous book, *My Way*.

2021 sees the publication of Kevin Moore's third book *Good Cop Bad Cop*, as well as *The Best of Times* by Eugene Barter and *Patron Saints of Gwent* by Christina Evans.

Join our mailing list at info@ saronpublishers.co.uk. We promise no spam ever.

Visit our website saronpublishers.co.uk to keep up to date and to read reviews of what we've been reading and enjoying. You can also enjoy the occasional offer of a free Bing chapter.

Follow us on Facebook @saronpublishing.
Follow us on Twitter @saronpublishers.

Notes

Preface

[1]   Funding from the Big Lottery Fund supported Second World War veterans, spouses, widows and carers to make commemorative trips to overseas Second World War battlesites.

[2]   John flew in Lancaster with No 15 Sqn. On the night of 12th September 1944, Lancaster NF958 (LS-M) of no 15 Sqn was lost in the skies above Mannheim when it was attacked by the Messerschmitt Bf110G-2 of Ofw Ludwig Schmidt of II/NGJ 6, the bomber receiving hits to the bomb bay which ignited the incendiaries still in their racks. Five of the crew bailed out and were taken prisoner. The pilot, F/O Norman Overend RNZAF, did not escape the aircraft. Flt Sgt Harry A Beverton was seen to leave the stricken Lancaster but was not seen again.

[3]   Reunions, at the Mildenhall Hotel, were initially set up by John and George, who paid for the meal at the start, as they were better off than most of the others.

New Owner

[1]   Others 'paid' only 12 cigarettes for their diaries.

Shot Down

[1]   He was stationed at Mildenhall in Suffolk.

[2]   The crew of the Lancaster LS-M consisted of F/O Norman Overend RNZAF; Sgt Barry J Howarth (survived); Sgt George B Thompson (survived); Flt Sgt John D Jones (survived); Flt

Sgt Robert PE Kendall (survived); Flt Sgt Harry A Beverton; Sgt I Spagatner (survived).

3   This was their 19th operation, though Sgt I Spagatner (Spag), who was the rear gunner, had only recently joined them. There was a philosophy, often proved to be unreliable, which said that on your first operation, there was a 1 in 20 possibility of being shot down. After five operations, that became a 1 in 5 chance, increasing to a 1 in 2 chance after your 10th operation.

4   Three hundred and ninety eight Lancasters were detailed to bomb Frankfurt's central station and rail lines. It was the last major attack of the war on Frankfurt. Seventeen aircraft were lost that night – of the 124 aircrew shot down, there were only ten survivors and five came from John's crew.

5   Bombers were much slower than fighters, and heavily-laden. Thus the Corkscrew Manoeuvre was designed to present the bomber to the fighter in a manner that the fighter would line up for attack and at the moment the attack began, the direction and altitude of the bomber would be violently changed through a series of direction and altitude changes.

6   A blockbuster bomb or cookie was any of several of the largest conventional bombs used in the Second World War. The term 'blockbuster' was originally a name coined by the press and referred to a bomb which had enough explosive power to destroy an entire street or large building through the effects of blast in conjunction with incendiary bombs.

My Diary Starts

1   Cigarettes became the preferred medium of exchange within the camps. They were also used to bribe German guards to provide the prisoners with outside items that would otherwise have been unavailable to them. Tins of coffee, hard to come by in Germany late in the war, served this same purpose in many camps. Contents of these Red Cross packages were

sometimes pilfered by German guards or other camp personnel, especially toward the end of the war.

Found and Interrogation

1. Buried his parachute.

2. Possibly for use as toilets on the train.

3. Rail Traffic Office.

4. Dulag Luft were POW transit camps, whose main purpose was to act as collection and interrogation centres for newly captured aircrew, before they were transferred to permanent camps. The main centre used was at Oberursel near Frankfurt. A satellite camp at Wetzlar was set up later to help cope with the large numbers of aircrew captured as the bombing campaign intensified against Germany. Allegations of interrogation under torture have been made by numerous POWs who passed through the camps.

5. This reference is to his wife Pat and baby daughter Mair.

6. Members of the Glider Pilot Regiment captured at the Battle of Arnhem in September 1944.

Wetzlar

1. A satellite camp set up later in the war to process RAF personnel.

2. Red Cross parcels, containing food, tobacco and personal items, were sent by the International Red Cross to Prisoners Of War. About 163,000 parcels were made up each week during the Second World War. The UK produced 20 million, Canada 16.5 million, while the American Red Cross contributed 27 million. Parcels also came from New Zealand, India, Argentina and S Africa. Parcels were sent to central collection points and transported, often in great danger, to the International Red Cross' headquarters in Geneva, from where

they were distributed to the camps. These packages augmented the often-meagre and deficient diets in the camps, contributing greatly to prisoner survival and an increase in morale. Sometimes, due to the shortage of parcels, two or even four prisoners would be compelled to share the contents of one Red Cross parcel.

Recipients were permitted to keep only the cigarettes and chocolate bars; the remainder of the parcel was turned over to the camp cook, who combined them with the contents of other parcels and German POW rations (usually bread, barley, potatoes, cabbage and horse meat) to create daily meals for the prisoners. The Scottish Red Cross parcels were the only ones to contain rolled oats.

3 Treet was a canned meat product similar to Spam. Sold as 'spiced luncheon loaf', it is made with chicken and pork and has a more finely ground texture than Spam, more akin to bologna or vienna sausages.

4 The camp was opened on 6th June 1944, for RAF NCO flying crews and by July held 230 prisoners. They were joined by members of the Glider Pilot Regiment captured at Arnhem in September 1944. By 1st January 1945, the camp held 1,578 prisoners. This was made up of 1,075 British, 252 Canadian, 134 Australian, 26 New Zealand, 24 French, 15 Polish, 14 South African, 11 Irish and 10 US. Others were Rhodesian, Maltese, Dutch, Belgian and Czech.

Bankau

1 The UK was seen as an unsuitable location for air training, due to the possibility of enemy attack and the unpredictable weather, so the British Commonwealth Air Training Plan, or Riverdale Agreement, was signed by the UK, Canada, Australia and New Zealand. This called for the training of

nearly 50,000 aircrew each year. By the end of the war, over 167,000 students had trained in Canada.

[2]   Street prostitutes who worked in Piccadilly Circus and the streets and alleys around Soho.

[3]   A popular hymn tune, written by John Hughes (1873-1932) in 1907. It is usually used in English as a setting for William Williams' text *Guide Me, O Thou Great Redeemer*.

[4]   Licentiate of the Royal Academy of Music.

[5]   A farce by the English playwright Ben Travers, the third of twelve Aldwych farces presented at the Aldwych Theatre between 1923 and 1933. The play depicts the complications that ensue when a young woman, dressed in pyjamas, seeks refuge from her bullying stepfather at a country house in the middle of the night.

[6]   From *The Princess: Sweet and Low* by Alfred, Lord Tennyson.

[7]   An English stage and film actor, humourist, singer, poet and monologist, famous for his comic and character roles, especially that of Alfred P. Doolittle in *My Fair Lady*.

[8]   The term 'dominion' means 'that which is mastered or ruled'. It was used by the British to describe their colonies or territorial possessions.

[9]   The Germans devised a ration that would keep Allied prisoners alive without breaking Germany's economic back: Each POW would receive 9 pounds of potatoes per week, augmented by 5 pounds of bread, and 2½ pounds of cabbage. Supplemental rations would include 7 ounces of sausage and small amounts of sugar, salt, barley and fake coffee, generally made from acorns after the tannins were leached. This potato-based diet was about as healthy as circumstances permitted, though it's doubtful that prisoners always got even these basic rations.

10 A 1928 dramatic play by R. C. Sherriff, set in an officers' dugout from 18th March 1918 to 21st March 1918.

11 A 1941 swashbuckler film starring Douglas Fairbanks Jr in a dual role as the title Siamese twins, separated at birth and raised in entirely different circumstances.

12 A 1941 American comedy and the 11th instalment of the sixteen popular Andy Hardy movies. It was also the last Andy Hardy movie to feature Judy Garland.

13 A 1943 American comedy. Intended as the first of a series, the film was not a success and the plans for sequels were scrapped.

14 British POWs were controlled by the Senior British Officer (SBO) or Senior British Non-Commissioned Officer (SBNCO). Some large camps had both a camp leader and a 'man of confidence' who was junior to him and handled any day-to-day negotiations with the Germans regarding, for example, camp routine, work schedules and diet. He reported directly to the International Committee of the Red Cross, responsible for inspecting camps and hospitals and producing reports. He could also be talked to in private.

15 A Welsh song and military march, traditionally said to describe events during the seven-year siege of Harlech Castle between 1461 and 1468. Commanded by Constable Dafydd ap Ieuan, the garrison withstood the longest known siege in the history of the British Isles. The song gained international recognition when it was featured in the 1941 movie *How Green Was My Valley* and the 1964 film *Zulu*.

16 A Welsh song sung to a tune first recorded in Edward Jones' *Musical and Poetical Relics of the Welsh Bards* (1784). The most commonly sung Welsh lyrics were written by John Ceiriog Hughes (1832-1887) and have been translated into several languages. The song is highly popular with traditional Welsh male voice choirs.

17 *Ton-y-Botel (Tune in a Bottle)* is a famous Welsh hymn tune composed by Thomas John Williams ATSC (1869–1944).

18 The Argentinian Red Cross provided parcels containing: 3 ounces bully beef, 5 ounces meat and vegs, 3 ounces ragout, 2 ounces corned mutton, 4 ounces port and beans, 5 ounces butter, 2 ounces lard, 2 ounces honey, 5 ounces jam, 2 ounces milk jam, 4 ounces condensed milk, 8 ounces sugar, 7 ounces cheese, 8 ounces biscuits.

19 A Canadian (1916-2003), he served in the RCAF, including seven months as a POW. He worked with the Boys Clubs of Canada and the William Roper Hull Residential Treatment Centre for Adolescents (Calgary) and became well-known for his intense and passionate love of music.

20 The scientific study of human sexuality, including human sexual interests, behaviours and functions.

21 George, John's friend, doesn't recall any serious tunnel work, though they did use the earth from one tunnel to build an ice skating rink for the Canadians, without the Germans knowing the earth came from the tunnel. Having an ice skating rink at a camp would have been unusual but obviously didn't trigger German suspicions.

22 9th January 1945 – evacuation from Stalag Luft 7 began in blizzard conditions. Fifteen hundred prisoners were force marched, then loaded onto cattle trucks and taken to Stalag III-A at Luckenwalde, south of Berlin.

23 A Luftwaffe-run POW camp, which held captured Western Allied air force personnel. Established in March 1942 in Lower Silesia near the town of Sagan (now Zagań, Poland), 160 kilometres (100 miles) south-east of Berlin, it was selected because its sandy soil made it difficult for POWs to escape by tunnelling. It is best known for two escape plots, one in 1943 that became the basis of a fictionalised film, *The Wooden Horse*

(1950), based on a book by escapee Eric Williams. The second breakout–the so-called Great Escape –of March 1944, was depicted in the film *The Great Escape* (1963), based on a book by former prisoner Paul Brickhill. The camp was liberated by Soviet forces in January 1945.

24   Nickname for the Russians, possibly from Joseph Stalin?

25   This referred to a hidden radio on which they listened to the news. John used this in case the Germans read the log book.

The Long March

1   The March refers to a series of forced marches during the final stages of the Second World War. As the Soviet Army was advancing on the Eastern Front, German authorities decided to evacuate POW camps, to delay liberation of the prisoners. From a total of 257,000 POWs held in Germany, over 80,000 were forced to march westward across Poland, Czechoslovakia and Germany in extreme winter conditions, between January and April 1945. The groups would march 20 to 40 kilometres a day – resting in factories, churches, barns and even in the open. Soon long columns of POWs were wandering over the northern part of Germany with little or nothing in the way of food, clothing, shelter or medical care.

On 19th January 1945, 1,500 prisoners marched out of Bankau in bitter cold. They crossed a bridge over the river Oder on 21st January, reached Goldberg on 5th February, and were loaded onto a train. On 8th February they reached Stalg III-A, located about 52 km (32 mi) south of Berlin near Luckenwalde, which already held 20,000 prisoners, consisting mainly of soldiers from Britain, Canada, the US and Russia.

Prisoners from different camps had different experiences: sometimes the Germans provided farm wagons for those unable to walk. There seldom were horses available, so teams of POWs pulled the wagons through the snow. Passing through some villages, the residents would throw bricks and stones, and in others, the residents would share their last food. With so little food they were reduced to scavenging to survive. Some were reduced to eating dogs and cats – and even rats and grass – anything they could obtain. Already underweight from years of prison rations, some were at half their pre-war body weight by the end. Because of the unsanitary conditions and a near starvation diet, hundreds died along the way and many more were ill. Dysentery was common: the Red Cross estimated that 80% of POWs were suffering from it. Sufferers had the indignity of soiling themselves whilst having to continue to march. Many suffered from frostbite which could lead to gangrene. Typhus was also a risk but was now increased by using overnight shelter previously occupied by infected groups. Some men simply froze to death in their sleep.

In addition to these conditions were the dangers from air attack by Allied forces mistaking the POWs for retreating columns of German troops.

It was later estimated that a large number of POWs had marched over 800 km (500 mi) by the time they were liberated, and some had walked nearly 1,500 km (930 mi).

2   Official figures estimate that about 1% of POWs died on these marches.

3   Those with intact boots had the dilemma of whether to remove them at night – if they left them on, trench foot could result; if they removed them, they may not get their swollen feet back into their boots in the morning or get frostbite. Worse still, the boots may freeze or, more likely, be stolen.

4   January and February 1945 were among the coldest winter months of the 20th century in Europe, with blizzards and temperatures as low as –25C (–13F), and even until the

middle of March, temperatures were well below 0C (32F). Most of the POWs were ill-prepared for the evacuation, having suffered years of poor rations and wearing clothing ill-suited to the appalling winter conditions.

5   Near the border with what is now the Czech Republic.

6   John had very bad arthritis later in life but it's not sure if it could be blamed on this period. However, he had an ankle injury from the parachute jump and land and because it wasn't seen to properly at the time, he had a disability pension for it.

Luckenwalde

1   Designed to hold 10,000 men, it was considered a model for other camps. Forty-three thousand French POWs arrived in mid-1940 and remained the largest group of prisoners until the end of the war. In 1941, some 300 of these took part in the Nazi propaganda film *Germanin*. In late 1944, small numbers of American, Romanian, British and Polish prisoners arrived. More than 200,000 prisoners passed through the Stalag III-A, and at its height in May 1944, there were a total of 48,600 POWs registered there. In February 1945, prisoners from Stalag III-B Furstenberg were evacuated to Stalag III-A, adding to the already overcrowded and unhygienic conditions. Finally, as the Russians approached, the guards fled the camp leaving the prisoners to be liberated by the Red Army on 22nd April 1945. Stalag III-A remains an example of poor conduct on the part of the Germans towards prisoners of war.

2   Varteg lies near Abersychan on the hills above the valley of the Afon Llwyd, between Pontypool and Blaenafon.

3   Ferrets were the guards who went into the huts while the POWs were on parade. They were searching for contraband and signs of escape plans/tunnels etc.

This was the word John used. He could have meant 'collaborate' or 'co-operate'.

A German boxer who was heavyweight champion of the world between 1930 and 1932, the only boxer to win the world heavyweight championship on a foul. After Hitler took over control in Germany, Schmeling, although he never joined the NSDAP, came to be viewed as a Nazi puppet and Hitler's chosen Aryan ideal. His two fights with Joe Louis in 1936 and 1938 were worldwide cultural events because of their national associations. During the war, Schmeling served with the Luftwaffe as an elite paratrooper (Fallschirmjäger). Long after the war, it was revealed that he had risked his life to save the lives of two Jewish children in 1938.

Klim was a dehydrated whole-milk powder used in the Tropics, where ordinary milk tended to spoil quickly. It soon became a staple of scientific explorers, geologists, soldiers, and other jungle travellers. Klim was later issued by the Red Cross to POWs, particularly those held in German prison camps, in order to increase caloric intake. Early ads featured the slogan 'Spell it backwards'.

March 5th was indeed a Monday, so this should read 'Tuesday March 6th' etc. John had got his dates somewhat muddled by this point.

De Havilland Mosquito bombers flew at high speed in medium and low altitude. They did daylight missions against factories, railways and other pinpoint targets in Germany and German-occupied Europe.

'Water crossing' refers to the Allied armies crossing the Rhine, which occurred on 7th March initially and unexpectedly. The POWs would have known about this from the 'Cocoa'.

Operation Plunder, involving a million men, was a military operation to cross the Rhine on the night of 23rd March 1945.

Preparations such as accumulation of supplies, road construction, and the transport of thirty-six Royal Navy landing craft, were hidden by a massive smoke screen from 16th March.

Liberation Day and Beyond

[1]   Gefanger = prisoner.

[2]   POWs called themselves 'Kreigies', short for the German word for POW, Kriegesgefangenen.

Printed in Great Britain
by Amazon